Ziyaret Tepe

Ziyaret Tepe

Exploring the Anatolian frontier
of the Assyrian Empire

CORNUCOPIA
BOOKS

Authors

Timothy Matney
University of Akron
John MacGinnis
Cambridge University
Dirk Wicke
University of Frankfurt
Kemalettin Köroğlu
Marmara University

With contributions by
Ian J. Cohn,
Tina Greenfield,
Britt Hartenberger,
Alex Hirtzel,
Hilary McDonald,
Willis Monroe,
Paola Pugsley,
Melissa Rosenzweig
and Mary Shepperson

Contents

9

0 5

cm

Acknowledgements

This book tells the story of an archaeological project carried out over many summers at the site of Ziyaret Tepe in the Diyarbakır Province of southeastern Turkey.

The project would not have been possible without the support of our generous sponsors. In particular, it is a deep honour to record our gratitude to the Tekfen Foundation and to Erhan Öner and Feyyaz Berker for their personal support. We cannot find words sufficient to express our thanks and the debt we owe them. Put simply, without this support the project could not have come through to its conclusion, let alone with such superlative results, and have been so productive in advancing our knowledge and understanding of this part of ancient Anatolia.

It has been a voyage of discovery. From the early years when the team was getting to know the land and the people, through many seasons of hard work under the hot Anatolian sun, it has been a privilege to work as part a team drawing its members from both Turkey and many countries further afield, united in their goal of striving to recover as much as possible of this exceptional site in the time available.

It has been a time of great discoveries and wonderful comradeship. It is a very great pleasure to record our profound thanks to everyone at Tekfen who has helped make this possible: first and foremost, to Erhan Öner and Feyyaz Berker for their personal generosity and belief in the project; to the Tekfen Foundation, and in particular to its chairman, Ercan Kumcu, for the further support which helped make this vision a reality; to Dori Kiss Kalafat for her unfailing patience and ingenuity and good humour in steering the project through many channels; to Esra Tüzgiray Kılıç for all her help; to Ian J. Cohn, Tina Greenfield, Britt Hartenberger, Alex Hirtzel, Hilary McDonald, Willis Monroe, Paola Pugsley, Melissa Rosenzweig and Mary Shepperson, who contributed directly to this publication, and to all the members of the team; to Erhan Öner, Kemalettin Köroğlu and Manuel Çıtak, and to the Museum of Anatolian Civilisations in Ankara, the Diyarbakır Museum, the trustees of the British Museum and the Ziyaret Tepe Archaeological Project for generously supplying images and the permission to use them; to Clive Crook and Debi Angel for their wonderfully creative setting of the book, and to Hilary Stafford-Clark for her meticulous editing of the manuscript; to Sabrina Klein for her creation of maps; and to everyone else who has played a part, large or small, in turning this great enterprise into such a resounding success.

'More students should be trained in archaeology and greater care should be taken over the exploration of the works and matchless treasures of ancient civilisations buried in almost all corners of our country, over their scientific preservation and classification, and over the restoration of monuments fallen into ruin due to the persistent neglect of previous generations.'

Mustafa Kemal Atatürk
March, 1931

Chapter 1
The origins of Assyria and its culture

Southeastern Turkey was home to some of the most important transitions in human existence. Among the earliest evidence for the domestication of plants and animals – the basis of humanity's food supply – comes from this region at sites such as Çayönü, Hallan Çemi, Nevalı Çori and Cafer Höyük, and from the mountain slopes of the Karacadağ. The world's earliest 'temple' is found in the monumental upright orthostats of Göbekli Tepe. Thousands of years before the Assyrians this region was productive farmland where inhabitants practised a mixed economy of growing cultivated wheat, barley and other vegetables and fruit, and herding flocks of sheep and goats, cattle and pigs. Ancient diets were supplemented with nuts, wild berries and abundant wild game such as gazelle.

It is hardly surprising that the landscape is dotted with hundreds of archaeological remains. During the Assyrian period, southeastern Turkey remained an important agricultural region and the productivity of the land was probably increased using irrigation canals in the fields around Ziyaret Tepe (though we lack direct evidence for these).

Two main elements of the physical

Left The upper Tigris, easternmost of Mesopotamia's two great rivers, the second being the Euphrates. From Turkey's southeastern mountains, the Tigris flows from west to east across 400km of Turkish territory, before turning south into Iraq and heading towards the Persian Gulf

geography were of prime importance to ancient peoples. First, the Tigris River and its tributaries were naturally the source of much of the water used for drinking, irrigation and other purposes in antiquity. The broad, flat floodplain surrounding the Tigris for much of its course through the Diyarbakır region is wide and the soils deposited by periodic flooding of the river are rich and fertile. The river served as a transportation corridor for moving materials, especially timber, downstream. A limited number of crossing points in antiquity meant that while movement from side to side of the river was possible, the physical presence of the wide Tigris was strategically important to the military. In fact, it was such an ordeal for the king's army to cross the river that chronicles often recount the number of times the army had to cross in pursuit of enemies.

The second key physical feature of the region was the Taurus Mountains to the north. The mountains were a source of important materials used in antiquity, most notably timber, stone and metal ore. The area of Ergani Maden, north of Diyarbakır, was an important copper mine and Kestel was the site of an ancient tin mine. These two elements were alloyed to make bronze.

Cuneiform texts from early in the

2nd millennium BC, found on the Anatolian plateau at the site of Kültepe, document a flourishing Assyrian trading colony in which Assyrian merchants exchanged tin and textiles, some from as far away as Babylonia (southern Iraq) and Iran, for silver and gold mined in the hills around Kültepe. By the time Ziyaret Tepe was part of the Assyrian Empire, as the provincial capital, Tušhan, these trading colonies were gone, replaced by a tribute system in which surrounding regions were either periodically raided by the Assyrian military, or were subjected to Assyrian tribute and taxes. In both cases, the goal was for the Assyrians to secure resources that were absent or scarce in their homelands: timber, stone and metal.

When we look at most ancient maps, the Assyrian Empire is usually represented as a solid mass of colour, suggesting that

Right Bas-relief from the palace of Ashurnasirpal in Nimrud showing Assyrian soldiers crossing a river on inflated goatskins

Below Topographical map showing Ziyaret Tepe's location between the Anatolian Mountains and the Mesopotamian plain

imperial control was uniform across vast distances. In reality, the landscape was much more varied. First of all, there was a large number of ethnic groups, seen for example in the range of languages spoken. Some of these groups would have identified themselves as Assyrians, but many would not. These included the Shubrians, living in the hills north of the Tigris River, who were an indigenous people prior to the arrival of the Assyrian imperial forces. They would have included various Aramean groups, some of whom are well-attested historically, such as the Bit Zamani of Diyarbakır. Others were deportees, brought to the region after their homelands were conquered by the Assyrians. These deportees farmed the land and worked to support the Assyrian administration. The Assyrians established fortified strongpoints; in addition to the

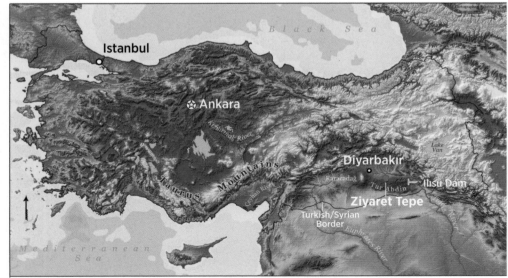

SABRINA KLEIN

Left The ancient black basalt walls of the city of Diyarbakır, one of southeastern Turkey's largest cities

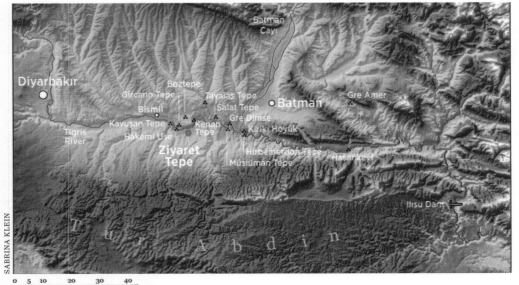

Left The area around Ziyaret Tepe, showing the main sites, rivers and towns

SABRINA KLEIN

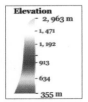

Elevation
— 2,963 m
— 1,471
— 1,192
— 913
— 634
— 355 m

city of Tušhan at Ziyaret Tepe, the sites of Pornak (Sinabu) and Üçtepe (Tidu) were also large fortified settlements on the Tigris River.

As one moved away from the river, however, Assyrian control waned and the countryside would have been dotted by the villages of indigenous Iron Age peoples. These people were also farmers and herders, and although they are not well known archaeologically, we see evidence of trade and influence with the established Assyrian centres.

Assyria

Assyria was a political state centred on the middle stretches of the river Tigris (now in modern Iraq). It was named after its original capital, the ancient city of Assur, whose roots go deep in prehistory. Assur was a worthy first capital: benefitting from its strategic position overlooking the Tigris, it could control communication with both the nomads of the Mesopotamian steppes and the rich agricultural land to the north. Assur also served as a nodal point in the trade of tin and bronze, with entrepôts in southeastern Anatolia.

Nevertheless, the origins of the Assyrian state are obscure. Glimpses from cuneiform sources indicate that in the latter part of the 3rd millennium BC the area fell under the control of the neighbouring Akkadian and then Ur III Empires. Assur gained independence following the collapse of the Ur III dynasty. The ensuing period was characterised by the famous trading colonies in Anatolia, but we know little of the political history.

This changed dramatically when, in the late 19th century BC, Assur was incorporated into the northern Mesopotamian Empire created by the Amorite leader Shamshi-Adad. Assyria then continued as an independent state until it was annexed by Saustatar, the king of Mitanni (a major international power centred around what is now northeastern Syria), sometime in the mid-15th century BC. Assyria only really began to find its role after it threw off Mitanni domination sometime shortly after 1400 BC. This paved the way for the empire of the Middle Assyrian period (c. 15th–11th centuries BC). Clay tablets found at Tell el-Amarna in Egypt contain diplomatic missives between the Assyrian king and the Egyptian Pharaoh Akhenaten, indicating that Assyria was now part of an international community.

After a period of contraction, in the Neo-Assyrian period (911–612 BC) Assyria began to expand once again, setting it on a road to becoming the greatest empire the world had ever seen. A succession of strong Assyrian kings campaigned in Turkey, Iran, southern Iraq (ancient Babylonia) and the Levant (the area of Lebanon, Israel, Jordan, the Palestinian territories and Syria). A network of provinces was established stretching across the Near East. Each province was under the control of a governor whose duties included collection of taxes and conscription of the local population. Assyria was a deeply complex civilisation. Even its capital city

Right Detail from a tablet found in the palace at Ziyaret Tepe recording, in cuneiform writing, women with names belonging to a previously unknown language (see page 96)
Below The extent of the Assyrian Empire

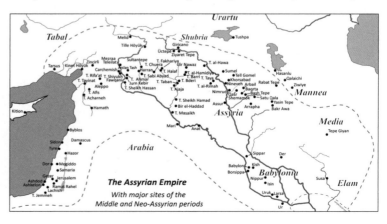

The Assyrian Empire
With major sites of the Middle and Neo-Assyrian periods

18

changed four times: Assur was followed by Nimrud, Khorsabad and, finally, Nineveh.

Assyria was also highly sophisticated, with each capital characterised by monumental palaces, temples and the mansions of the elite, all decorated with sculptures, painting and textiles. A great deal of our knowledge about Assyria comes thanks to its copious written records. The Assyrian language was written in Mesopotamian cuneiform (wedge-shaped) script, using hundreds of characters. The Assyrians mostly wrote on clay tablets, though waxed writing boards were also used for temporary records that needed continual updating, such as lists of soldiers and registers of income and expenditure. From at least the 9th century BC, Aramaic (the language of Jesus) began to be used. It was written in an alphabetic script on parchment, potsherds, and as epigraphs on clay tablets.

Cuneiform script

After a long and interesting prehistory, writing emerged in southern Mesopotamia a little before 3000 BC. At first pictographic, the method of writing on clay with a triangular reed soon led to the evolution of true cuneiform (wedge-shaped) writing. The script was then in use until the 1st century AD, a period of more than 3,000 years. From its origins as an administrative tool, cuneiform came in the fullness of time to be used for writing all manner of texts: letters, contracts, royal inscriptions, literature, prayers, rituals, astronomical texts and so on. An early instance of cuneiform writing in Anatolia may be found in the inscribed monument of Naram-Sin from Pir Hussein, 25km east of Diyarbakır, which dates to the later 3rd millennium BC. But in Turkey the use of the script really took off in the early 2nd millennium BC with the appearance of the Old Assyrian commercial colonies.

From the entrepôt at Kültepe, ancient Kaneš, in Kayseri province, and from other sites, tens of thousands of texts have been recovered documenting the trade of merchants operating from their base at Assur, nearly 800km away on the Tigris in northern Iraq. Cuneiform was subsequently adopted by the Hittite Empire and used over a period of almost 400 years, from approximately 1550 to 1180 BC, for writing both Hittite itself as well as lesser-known languages such as Hurrian and Hattic. At this time the Hittite kings – like the Assyrian kings – even corresponded in cuneiform with the Pharaoh in Egypt. Under the Urartian Empire (9th–6th centuries BC) cuneiform was also adapted to the writing of Urartian.

The expansion of the Assyrian Empire into Anatolia has left us stelae such as those found at Zincirli and Kurkh (Üçtepe), both inscribed and uninscribed rock reliefs, and tablets from around a dozen sites. The latest cuneiform inscriptions from Turkey currently known are the stelae of Nabonidus from Harran, south of Urfa, which date to the mid-6th century BC.

The environmental overview

Left
The magnificent
mound of
Ziyaret Tepe,
which lies in
the Diyarbakır
basin, viewed
from the south

Ziyaret Tepe is located in the upper Tigris River valley in southeastern Turkey, at approximately 500–550m above sea level, in a geographic area referred to as the Diyarbakır Basin. This valley runs west to east and is bounded by the Taurus mountain range to the north and east, the Mardin plateau to the south and the isolated peaks created by tectonic activity around the Karacadağ volcano (now dormant) to the west. Ancient inhabitants of Ziyaret Tepe would have enjoyed the site's access to the Tigris River and would have grown their crops in the rich alluvial soils of the river's floodplain. The landscape would also have supported pastoral practices, the Diyarbakır Basin being a semi-arid region with steppe vegetation suitable for grazing animal herds in the surrounding low foothills that border the river.

The semi-arid climate in the Diyarbakır Basin today is similar to that which the people of Ziyaret Tepe would have experienced 3,000 years ago. The summer months (June–September) would have been very hot and dry, with temperatures regularly hovering around 40°C and very little rainfall. Most of the year's precipitation would come in the cold winter months. Rain would fall between December and February, when temperatures could drop to well below freezing.

In order to find trees for construction and fuel, the people of Ziyaret Tepe could harvest the species that grew along the river bank, such as poplar, willow and tamarisk. But the best source of wood would have been the forests of the lower Taurus Mountains, up to hundreds of kilometres away, which contained oak, juniper and pine trees.

GAP and the Ilısu Dam, the project that has prompted so many excavations in the area

Above The Ilısu Dam under construction

The choice of Ziyaret Tepe as the location of our project was determined by both archaeological research questions and modern Turkish politics. In the 1930s the Turkish authorities started formulating a plan, known as the GAP plan, for dozens of hydroelectric dams to be built along the Euphrates and Tigris Rivers and their tributaries, with the goal of providing both electricity and irrigation water to the southeastern part of the country. The site of one of these dams near the modern village of Ilısu, approximately 150km downstream from Ziyaret Tepe, was determined in the mid-1970s. In the early 1990s the Turkish Ministry of Culture put out a call for international archaeological research teams to work in the region to be

Above Hasankeyf, with its Roman bridge
Right The village of Halfeti, by Lake Birecik
Below Open canals bring in the water needed to irrigate farmland

impacted by the creation of a reservoir that will cover over 300sq km of land and flood hundreds of archaeological sites.

Prof. Timothy Matney, from the University of Akron, Ohio, was one of the first archaeologists to answer this call. In the winter of 1996 he requested a permit, which was granted, and our work started in the summer of 1997. Following many delays, the State Hydraulics Works started construction of the Ilısu Dam in the summer of 2006 and, as of 2016, work at Ilısu is still ongoing.

The mound at Ziyaret Tepe

Ziyaret Tepe is a prominent feature in the landscape of the upper Tigris River valley. The tall citadel mound, or *höyük*, rises 22m above the surrounding plain. With steep sides and a flattish top, the shape of the mound belies its human origin, being comprised of layers representing thousands of years of debris from human occupation. To the trained eye, the *höyük* is easily distinguishable from the gentle rolling and rounded hills of the upper Tigris River valley. Driving along the road starting in Diyabakır and following the course of the Tigris downstream, Ziyaret Tepe is first visible after one crests a major rise created by a relict gravel bar some 80m high and 6km west of the site. Because of its imposing size, the mound at Ziyaret Tepe has been well known to European scholars and is briefly described in mid-19th-century travellers' accounts. In fact, it is so prominent that the site is visible in photographic imagery made by US military CORONA satellites in the 1960s and 1970s.

In 2000, excavation started at Ziyaret

Previous pages
The mound at Ziyaret Tepe seen from the north, with the Tigris in the foreground

Right, below
Early black and white pictures of the excavation of the residence in Operation G

Left
Prof. Timothy Matney surveying using the 'total station'

Tepe and one of our first tasks was to determine the age and history of the settlement. Dr Michael Roaf, a professor at Munich University in Germany, directed a small team of students and local Turkish workmen to cut a 5m-wide trench from the top of the *höyük* to the base of the mound, a long, narrow slice that revealed layers covering thousands of years of human occupation. At the base Dr Roaf uncovered remains dating back to the beginning of the Early Bronze Age, roughly 3000 BC, and above this earliest settlement were occupational layers spanning the Middle and Late Bronze, and Early and Middle Iron Ages. In short, the *höyük* demonstrates nearly continuous occupation until 611 BC, when our Assyrian city was abandoned following the sack of the imperial capitals far away to the south in modern-day Iraq.

The mound, however, is only a part of ancient Ziyaret Tepe. Nearly 30 hectares of land to the east, west and south of the site were also inhabited during its Assyrian occupation. We call this area the 'lower town', although it was really part of a thriving urban city. The lower town was surrounded in the Assyrian period by tall fortification walls, supported by exterior towers and broken in at least two places by monumental gateways. Inside the city walls were public buildings and private residences, streets and large, open public courtyards. Although we have no direct evidence, Assyrian descriptions of other major cities suggest that there would have been canals, gardens, orchards and other green spaces within ancient Ziyaret Tepe.

Over the course of our 18 seasons of fieldwork at Ziyaret Tepe, we conducted a variety of surveys and excavations. The entire surface of the 32-hectare site was topographically mapped and we undertook a systematic surface survey, collecting pottery and other artefacts in order to determine the extent of the ancient habitations.

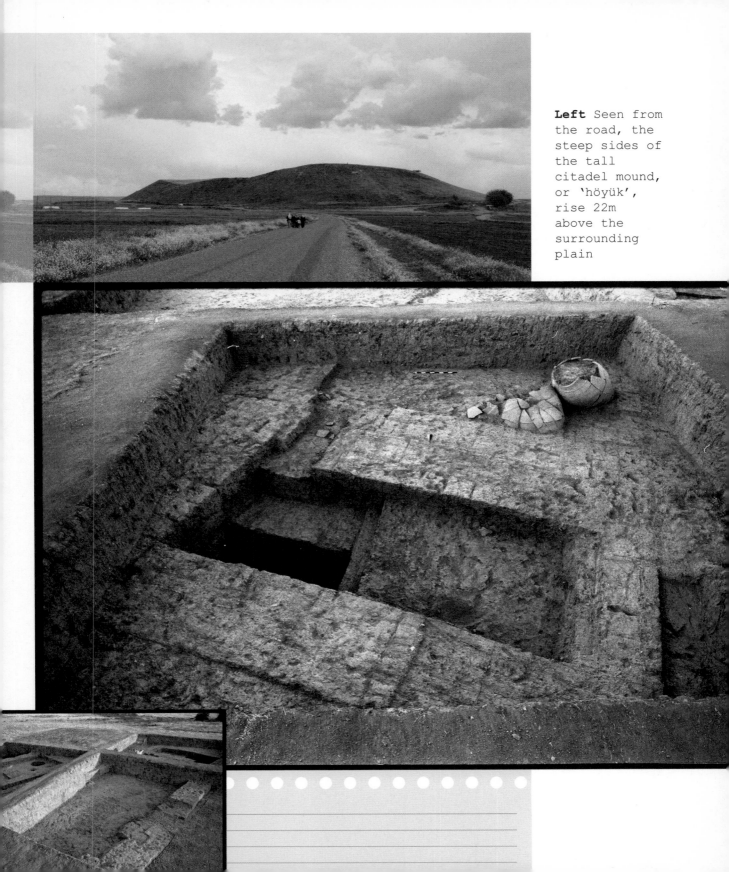

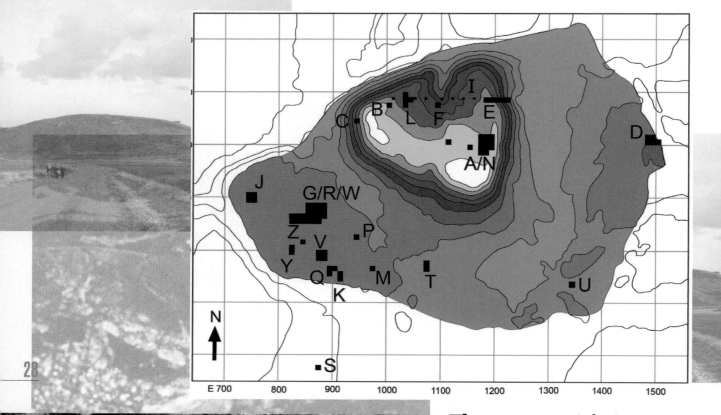

The operation areas

Over the course of the fieldwork we worked in many locations on both the high mound and in the lower town. Each excavation area was called an 'Operation' and designated with a letter, from Operation A all the way through to Operation Z. A summary of the full list of Operations is given in Appendix A. In two cases, when we returned to an area after a significant interval, the work was given a new designation: hence when the work in the palace (originally Operation A) was resumed it was given the designation Operation N, and when work was resumed in the lower town in the area of Operation G it was designated Operation R. These areas are often referred to as Operation A/N and G/R respectively.

Dating the occupation of the mound

One of the first tasks in approaching a new site is to establish when it was occupied. This starts before excavation with the collection of ceramics from the surface. In many cases the form, material and decoration can be diagnostic of a specific period. Other artefacts found on the surface can also give clues to dating – at Ziyaret Tepe this included Assyrian brick fragments and Roman roof tiles, while a Palaeolithic hand-axe hints at a much older human presence in the region.

Another important category is coins, which can often be dated to an exact year. One needs to be aware, though, that coins can stay in circulation for very long periods of time, meaning that the date of the coin may well not correspond to the date of the layer in which it is found. Also, because they are small, coins can be moved by plant growth and animal action, again meaning that they are in a displaced context. Cuneiform tablets can also sometimes be dated to an exact year, and failing that at least to an approximate period.

Lastly there are the scientific dating methods. These can be utilised once the excavation has progressed to the point that we can recover appropriate samples from contexts which are both reliable (not contaminated) and informative. The most common method remains radiocarbon dating, which we employed repeatedly. We also experimented with archaeomagnetic dating, a technique based on the fact that the alignment of the earth's magnetic field changes over time, although in this case it was to help researchers calibrate the curve.

Left, top
Topographical map of the site showing locations of the different excavation areas

Left, below
Satellite view of the region around Ziyaret Tepe. The red arrow indicates the location of the high mound, the yellow arrows the limits of the lower town

The abandonment of the city in the 11th century BC

At Ziyaret Tepe we have firm archaeological evidence for two discrete periods of Assyrian domination: the first during the Middle Assyrian period (c. 1300–1050 BC) and the second during the Late Assyrian period (at Ziyaret Tepe, 882–611 BC). During these times Ziyaret Tepe served as an administrative, military and commercial centre for the Empire. At some point during the mid-11th century BC, the city of Tušhum (as Tušhan was known then) was abandoned by the Assyrians. Their mud-brick buildings, now without constant upkeep and left exposed to the elements, quickly fell apart.

We can imagine that the fields turned to weeds, the irrigation canals began to silt up, and the once bustling city was mostly silent. When the Assyrians left, they would have taken their animals and portable possessions with them. Although some of the inhabitants of the city would have returned to Assyria, an inscription of King Ashurnasirpal II describes how in 882 BC he brought back the 'enfeebled Assyrians', who were scattered throughout the landscape, and rebuilt Tušhan. So it is clear that some of the inhabitants had moved into the hills and valleys surrounding the site during the century-and-a-half that the site was not under Assyrian control.

We have no clear evidence that people lived at Ziyaret Tepe during this long Assyrian hiatus. That said, in the archaeological strata between the Middle and Late Assyrian levels, there is evidence of human activities on the high mound. Most importantly, we see the presence of large pits in several places. These pits were 2–3m in diameter and were roughly 2m deep. They were cut into the Middle Assyrian levels (meaning that they are later in time than 1050 BC) and were sealed by the construction of the Late Assyrian buildings found above them (meaning that they predate 882 BC). Some archaeologists believe these Early Iron Age pits are the remains of semi-subterranean houses, but the ones found at Ziyaret Tepe have no evidence of having been lived in. Rather, they were most likely storage pits. One hypothesis that we have been exploring is that these pits may have been used by agro-pastoralists who collected grain during the late spring harvest and stored the cereals in underground pits for later consumption. This same technology is still in use in modern times and we were able to see the creation of enormous pits that were filled with wheat and covered first by plastic, and then by soil during years when harvests were especially plentiful and the usual silos were full. While the high mound was a good place for such activities, it appears that nobody lived here.

Who were these agro-pastoralists of the Early Iron Age? The few Assyrian texts found elsewhere during this interlude do not provide much direct evidence, but cuneiform texts from the 9th century BC make it clear that when Ashurnasirpal II and his contemporaries came to the region they found the local power structure dominated by local kings who spoke Aramaic. These Aramaean kingdoms became part of a complex power struggle in which Assyrian kings soon found themselves embroiled. It is at this time that the city of Tušhan was refounded and became the administrative capital of an important Assyrian border province.

Right
Most areas of the site have been cut by pits dug at later periods for either storage or disposal of refuse. Here we see work in the lower town, cotton fields in the background

Assyrian ethnic diversity

The Assyrian Empire was a melting-pot of peoples from across the Near East. In the heartland the majority were of course Assyrian, but even here the Assyrians were not the aboriginal population. Prior to the Assyrians the region had been home to the Hurrians, a people who occupied a swathe of territory across Syria, southeastern Turkey and northern Iraq. Around the end of the 2nd millennium BC we witness the arrival of the Arameans, infiltrating from the west and establishing in the process the 'Neo-Hittite' kingdoms, successor states filling the vacuum left by the collapse of the Hittite Empire. Whether through trade or war, there were also contacts with Urartu, Elam, Arabia and Egypt. There may even be other elements about which we have no information at all.

This ethnic diversity is reflected in the languages spoken. While Assyrian was the senior language of the administration – the letter of Mannu-ki-libbali (see pages 158 and 219) makes it clear that it was in use until the end – the language of the indigenous population was Shubrian, which may have been a dialect of Hurrian. Aramaic was certainly spoken – it was indeed the lingua franca of the Assyrian Empire – and also written (this, too, is indicated by Mannu-ki-libbali's letter), although we did not in fact recover any Aramaic inscriptions at Ziyaret Tepe.

Beyond this, there will have been the languages spoken by deportees moved into the province. As we will see, one group is thought to have come from the Zagros region, speaking a tongue which cannot so far be identified. Apart from the languages, all these constituents will have had their own religions and cultural traditions. A problem for archaeologists is that while there may be some material evidence for these different strands, the correlation of pottery types with cultural groups is fraught with difficulties, while some of the best markers of cultural affiliation – for example, food and clothing – may leave no trace in the archaeological record.

A long tradition of deportation

If there is one thing which characterised and fuelled the machinery of the Assyrian Empire, it was the practice of deportation. It was what oil is to the economy of today. While the practice of capturing and deporting prisoners of war stretches back as far as history – the very earliest proto-literate texts, from the late 4th millennium BC, already record prisoners brought down from the mountains – it was under the Neo-Assyrian kings that the practice reached its height.

Uprooting large numbers of indigenous populations and transplanting them across the Empire evolved into a premier tool of Assyrian rule. They were used like chess pieces in the game of imperial control. It became almost standard procedure when a new territory was invaded and annexed. Ashurnasirpal, for example, claimed after his defeat of Amme-ba'li of Bit Zamani: 'I uprooted 1,500 troops of the Ahlamû Arameans and brought them to Assyria.'

The rationale was twofold: the breaking-up of communities destroyed the pre-existing power structures of the indigenous society, while the newly transported people were entirely dependent on the Assyrian administration. At the same time, the flow of manpower could be directed into work on major agricultural and engineering projects. As

Above
Deportees escorted by soldiers. A bas-relief from the palace of Sennacherib in Nineveh

put by the famous Cambridge archaeologist David Oates: 'Mass deportation was initially an ingenious and, for the time, successful solution of two problems, the maintenance of control over territories larger than Assyria itself, and the provision, for the construction of the great cities, of labour forces greater than Assyria alone could furnish.'

It is certain that Tušhan was built and settled by deportees, and while we have no information on the origin of the first deportees transported to Tušhan by either Ashurnasirpal or Shalmaneser, we do know that a later Assyrian king, Tiglath-pileser III, deported 83,000 people from Hamath (modern Hama, on the Orontes river in western Syria) and settled them in the province. The epigrapher Simo Parpola has suggested that some of the names in the texts excavated at Ziyaret Tepe hint at descent from Babylonian deportees. Another text from the palace (see page 96) bears the names of 144 women thought to have been deported to the city from the Zagros Mountains.

The Assyrians in the northern territories

Until recently our knowledge of the Assyrians in the north came almost entirely from cuneiform sources. These texts indicate that a presence had been established along the upper Tigris in the Middle Assyrian period by Shalmaneser I (1274–1245 BC) but also that this did not last.

For our purposes, the story really begins with forays by Tukulti-Ninurta II (891–883 BC). This king campaigned in the area and successfully exacted tribute from Amme-ba'li, the local king of the Anatolian state of Bit Zamani (approximately the area of Diyarbakır). This renewed Assyrian involvement in the north, but it was left to the son of Tukulti-Ninurta II, Ashurnasirpal II (883–859 BC), to establish the Assyrian presence on firm foundations.

Ashurnasirpal campaigned here in his second and fifth years (882 and 879 BC), when a revolt of Amme-ba'li was brutally suppressed. This paved the way for Ashurnasirpal to implement a truly imperial agenda. In his own words: 'I repossessed the fortified cities of Tidu and Sinabu which Shalmaneser, king of Assyria, a prince who preceded me, had garrisoned and which the Arameans had captured by force. I resettled in their abandoned houses and cities the Assyrians who had held the fortresses of Assyria in the lands of Nairi and whom the Arameans had subdued. I placed them in a peaceful abode. I uprooted 1,500 troops of the Ahlamû Arameans belonging to Amme-ba'li, a man of Bit Zamani, and brought them to Assyria. I reaped the harvest of

Right
A sculpture of the Assyrian king Shalmaneser III carved into the cliff face at the Tigris Tunnel

Below left and centre
The Tigris Tunnel at Lice

Below right A bronze strip from the gates of the temple at Balawat, near Nimrud in Iraq, showing an Assyrian attack on towns in Shubria

the Nairi lands and stored it for the sustenance of my land in the cities Tušha, Damdammusa, Sinabu and Tidu.'

Subsequently Ashurnasirpal's son Shalmaneser III (858–824 BC) campaigned in Syria and southeastern Turkey, strengthening Assyrian control and also exacting tribute from Shubria, the kingdom across the Tigris directly north of Tušhan. From this time the Tigris at Tušhan formed the northern border of the Assyrian Empire, a situation which continued until 673 BC, a period of over two hundred years. In that year the Assyrian King Esarhaddon (680–669 BC) invaded across the Tigris, annexing Shubria and dividing it into the two new provinces of Uppumu and Kullimeri. With the border pushed further north, Tušhan became an internal part of the Empire and appears to have remained stable until the end.

Outpost of the Roman Empire

Although Ziyaret Tepe was a large city only under the Assyrian Empire, we found archaeological evidence of a number of other groups living at the site, both long before and long after the Assyrians. For example, during the 4th–6th centuries AD, Ziyaret Tepe was occupied by a group of Roman farmers, who built a modest number of domestic buildings in the southern lower town. We don't know the Roman name for the settlement and Ziyaret Tepe did not play an important role in the political fortunes of the Empire. Nevertheless, excavations in the lower town provide a useful insight into the daily life of commoner peasants living in Roman Anatolia.

Historians Beate Dignas and Engelbert Winter describe the upper Tigris River valley during the 4th–6th centuries AD as a borderland between two powerful imperial traditions: the Romans and Byzantines to the west and the Sassanians to the east. At Diyarbakır the earliest city walls were constructed by the Romans in the late 3rd century AD, following the peace treaty in 298 AD between Diocletian

Above
Coin of Constantius II (337–361 BC)

Right
A juglet of the Late Roman period

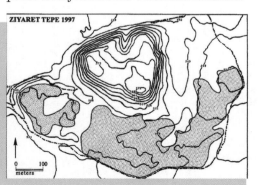

Left
Map showing the distribution of Late Roman ceramics across the site

and the Sassanian king Narse, and the area immediately east of the Tigris, an area called Trans-Tigritania, was ceded to Rome. The Tigris River, according to Roman texts, formed the de facto border between the two powers, although there were periodic incursions of Sassanians. For example, Amida (Diyarbakır) was captured briefly three times by them.

Archaeological surveys support the general picture painted by the Roman texts, and important Roman fortifications and settlements are well documented along the frontier (at Çattepe, Fenik and Semrah Tepe), forming what Guillermo Algaze and his survey team called a 'chain of fortified outposts along the border'. Excavations at Ziyaret Tepe in three places – Operations J, T and U – revealed the presence of two superimposed layers of architecture dating to the Late Roman period. The architecture comprises stone wall foundations, above which would have stood mud-brick walls.

One class of artefact of this period found ubiquitously at Ziyaret Tepe is large terracotta roof tiles, typical of the Roman period. We reconstruct the Late Roman settlement of Ziyaret Tepe to have a small number of such buildings spread across the southern lower town, with a population of maybe 100 people or even fewer. These were not the wealthy villas that one usually pictures when one thinks of Roman houses, but rather well-built farmhouses from which the Romans worked the rich agricultural lands of the Tigris River floodplain.

Our dating for the Roman levels comes primarily from its artefacts: pottery, roof tiles, small objects typical of Roman manufacture, and, importantly, coins. These are unusual artefacts in that their manufacture is datable to a span of a few years as the details of their design and minting changed with the political fortunes of the Roman leaders. Of course, it is likely that most coins were in circulation for

Above
Late Roman roof tiles

Right
The Late Roman levels of
Operation T

Below
Fragment of a Late Roman
'pilgrim flask', or
water bottle

years, probably decades, before they were
dropped or lost and became part of the
archaeological record. At Ziyaret Tepe all
the coins that we have found have been
single, isolated finds, suggesting that they
were accidently lost, not part of a hoard
deliberately buried to be retrieved later.

Far more common indicators of everyday
Roman life are pottery vessels found on the
earthen floors of Roman buildings, and
small fragments of glass vessels. Glass had
been invented almost a thousand years
before the traditional founding of Rome,
but in southeastern Turkey the discovery
of glass artefacts only becomes common
during the Roman period, when delicate
glass vessels and other small items were
widespread, even in villages such as
Ziyaret Tepe.

The medieval period

Long after the end of the Roman occupation of the site, farmers were once again attracted to the *höyük* of Ziyaret Tepe during the Middle Islamic period (12th–15th centuries AD). The Middle Islamic village at Ziyaret Tepe was a modest settlement of mud-brick houses and storerooms with intervening courtyard areas. Exact estimates are difficult to make, but we hypothesise that the population of the village was fewer than 150. The ancient name of the village during this period is lost to us and we know of no contemporary documentation describing it.

As noted by historian Peter Holt, in the Middle Islamic period the broad region became known as Diyar Bakr, abode of the tribe of Bakr, named after a tribe that settled here after the Muslim conquest in the 7th century. In the Middle Islamic period the principal dynastic power in the upper Tigris River valley was the Artuqid dynasty, a ruling clan of an important group of Turcomans who came to the area in the early 11th century after suffering military setbacks in Palestine and western Syria. They acquired the cities of Mardin and Hasankeyf and remained a significant regional power until the early 15th century. In addition to the Artuqids, the political history of this region is complex and Seljuk, Ayyubid, Mongol, Mamluk and Aq Qoyunlu dynasts also played important

Below
Medieval signet ring with a stylised inscription

20 cm

roles prior to annexation by the Ottomans in the early 16th century.

Mehmet Mehdi Ilhan in his work *The 1518 Ottoman Cadastral Survey of the Sancak of Amid,* describes the area of Diyarbakır as 'overwhelmingly agricultural and pastoral' and fairly treeless, and he notes that large numbers of nomads in the region kept much potential agricultural land under pasturage. According to early-16th-century cadastral surveys, taxes were levied on cattle, hay, wheat, barley, millet and lentils. Similar conditions most probably prevailed in the Middle Islamic period and we see this

few interesting artefacts that show connections between medieval Ziyaret Tepe and the big cities of Diyarbakır, Mardin and Hasankeyf. These include beautifully glazed polychrome pottery, a colourful glass bracelet fragment and a bronze ring with an inscription. All of these were probably made in and imported from the major centres. One particularly surprising discovery was the skull and long bones of a cow that had been buried in a foundation trench beneath the mud-brick walls of one of the buildings; we think that this was part of a votive or dedicatory offering.

Our current understanding is that the village of Ziyaret Tepe was abandoned in the 15th century, before the Ottoman conquest of the region. The 1518 Ottoman survey mentioned above notes that a small village called Depe Kendi sat near the location of the modern town of Tepe, 1.5km west of Ziyaret Tepe, but there is no mention of the ancient mound of Ziyaret Tepe being occupied. Here the historical and archaeological records are in agreement.

41

Above
Fragment of a
medieval glass
vessel

Left
A cow's skull
buried as a
foundation
deposit below
the wall of a
medieval house
in Operation L

region as prime farming and grazing land.

In the 12th–15th centuries AD, Ziyaret Tepe was not an important place politically, although the architectural and other remains found during our excavations suggest a prosperous farming community. In Operation L, Prof. Dr Kemalettin Köroğlu excavated over a dozen rooms, comprising at least three or four buildings centred around an open courtyard. While most of the finds from these buildings were plain ceramics, broken pieces of iron, animal bones and the remains of everyday life, we did find a

The Ottoman period

Earlier we noted that Ziyaret Tepe appears to have been abandoned prior to the Ottoman conquest of the early 16th century AD. In fact, one of the features of the *höyük* that struck us during the initial 1997 surface surveys was the general lack of Ottoman and modern remains, apart from two modern cemeteries which are still in use. One of these cemeteries sits on the southeastern corner of the high mound. Here a small shrine (*türbe*) was built several decades ago around the tomb of Sheikh Muhammad, a religious leader from Tepe. The second modern cemetery sits at the western base of the high mound, near the road leading to the *höyük*. During our summers at Ziyaret Tepe we witnessed a number of burials in both cemeteries as the local population from Tepe continued to use their traditional burial grounds.

A surprising find in 2006 was the discovery, just beneath the modern surface of the mound in Operation L, of linear arrangements of medium-sized stones forming several oval or circular features about 6m across at the widest point. The stones were held together in places with mud, although there was no evidence that mud bricks were employed. In fact, the stones were not really wall foundations, but possibly served to delineate the edge of temporary structures, possibly tents. Large flat stones found within the oval and circular features may have served as supports for wooden posts. Associated finds included hand-made pottery, a stamped clay prayer disk and fragments of clay tobacco pipes.

While this architectural stratum is very ephemeral, if our interpretation is correct then this may be one of the very few nomadic tent encampments recovered archaeologically in southeastern Turkey. It is impossible accurately to date this 'tent level', other than to say it is later than the Middle Islamic layers below. So this occupational level – the last known from Ziyaret Tepe – could date to anywhere from the 16th through to the early 20th century. In the mid-19th century, the English explorer J. G. Taylor noted that this area was home to many communities living in tents, and presumably such nomadic peoples have a long, largely invisible, history in the Diyarbakır region.

Above
Ottoman clay prayer disc

Right
Ottoman clay pipes

Far right
Map of the empire of Süleyman the Magnificent (*Courtesy of Erhan Öner*)

JUSTUS DANCKERUM 1680 49 X 57 CM, COPPERPLATE, COLLECTION NUMBER: ÖNER 282

Following local tradition, families sleep on the rooftops in the hot summer months

The village of Tepe

The majority of the workmen who laboured with us at Ziyaret Tepe came from the local village of Tepe. The village itself dates back to the Ottoman period, when it was called Behramki. In the 1845–1846 Ottoman census, Behramki and the surrounding villages were home to 1,459 households: 876 Muslim, 574 Christian and 9 Copt Muslim. Although the earlier history of Tepe may stretch back as far as the

16th century, the modern village of Tepe was only incorporated with its own municipal administration in 1992. The population in the early 1990s was just under 4,000 inhabitants, but by the time our project finished in 2014 that number had nearly tripled as the town prospered. Shortly before we left, Tepe was transferred under the administrative control of the city of Bismil, 13km upstream on the left bank of the Tigris River. During our project we worked with two different mayors (*belediye başkanı*) – Sebih Sümer and Ahmet Çelebi – both of whom showed enormous generosity and helped our team in numerous ways.

For millennia, long before even the Assyrians were in the valley, this region

Above, clockwise from top left
Strolling through the village of Tepe; Süleyman, owner of a local grocer's shop; a village girl descends a flight of stairs, passing rows of aubergines and peppers strung out to dry; Prof. Matney (right) presents a quilt embroidered in the colours of the Turkish flag to the mayor of Tepe, Sebih Sümer

was prime agricultural land. The most important agricultural crops have always been wheat and barley, and in fact some of the earliest evidence for the domestication of these crops comes from southeastern Turkey, dating back over 10,000 years. When we arrived in Tepe in 1997, wheat was the overwhelmingly dominant crop being grown by the villagers. Requiring no irrigation, only the winter rains, wheat planted in the autumn was harvested shortly before we arrived each summer for fieldwork. The fields of the lower town, many still with stubble waiting to be burned, were ideal for the large-scale excavations that we wanted to undertake. During July and August and into early September the fields turned from golden to black, following their annual burning to add nutrients to the soil, and then to a hard, dusty brown as very little grew in the intense summer heat.

From the early 2000s a new crop became increasingly popular, and the fields that had always been empty in the summer were increasingly planted with cotton. Extensive irrigation systems were required to grow the cotton crop, with gasoline-powered pumps used to draw water out of the Tigris River to holding basins at higher elevations. Irrigation water was released into the fields employing simple gravity-fed systems to water the plants. The fields around Ziyaret Tepe were, for the first time, a deep green well into the scorching summer, and the white bolls of the cotton

Above

A woman tends her tannur, or bread oven, as the sun rises in Tepe. Many houses will share communal bread ovens whose traditional design is found in the later archaeological contexts at Ziyaret Tepe

plant were ripe for picking in August.

The arrival of cotton affected our project in several ways. First, the fields that had normally been accessible to us were now often planted with cotton. The irrigation systems made some work, such as geophysical survey, impossible in places, and across the lower town there was damage to the underlying archaeological remains. In 2002 we arrived to find that a large iron irrigation pipe running from the Tigris River to the hills 2km distant to the south had been constructed over the mound. Protests from the Diyarbakır Museum's director to the Ministry of Culture in Ankara failed to have the pipe removed, and when we left in 2014 it was still in operation, although a

global drop in the price of cotton had forced many farmers to return to wheat production.

The village itself was of great interest to our team, as it opened up vistas to understanding both traditional and modern Turkish life. The tea houses, barber's shops, grocers and – in time – internet cafés were a welcome change from the dig-house and its unending supply of archaeological work. The main streets and public buildings were built with contemporary materials, equipped with air-conditioning and other amenities, while the private houses, set off the principal thoroughfares, still employed traditional mud-brick architecture with open courtyards and

Above, clockwise from top left
Collecting cotton during the harvest; an old grinding stone, powered by a mule, still in use at the beginning of our expedition; many houses have garden plots in their courtyards; the team relaxes at the village barber's shop

flat roofs where many daily activities
and crafts were still undertaken.

In the summer heat the villagers slept on
their roofs and started their day before
sunrise – cleaning, baking and cooking,
working the fields and gardens, until midday,
when the heat drove people indoors or into
the relative cool of the shade. We observed
shepherds with their flocks of sheep and
goats or small herds of cattle taking animals
out to graze in the mornings, returning in
the evening along the dusty village roads.
While the agriculture is thoroughly modern,
employing large tractors and harvesters,
some grain is still stored in underground pits
covered with earth. Much smaller ancient
storage pits were uncovered at Ziyaret Tepe,
linking past and present practice.

Above Workers
heading back to
the village at
lunchtime

Right Cleaning
cotton, fresh
from the
harvest

51

Chapter 2

The excavation team gets down to work

Left
The 2012 team
on the steps of
the dig-house in
Bismil
**Back row,
from left**
John MacGinnis,
Jordan Bell,
Lourdes Mesa
García, Hayley
Monroe, Charlie
Draper, Tina
Greenfield, Azer
Keskin, Paola
Pugsley, Fabian
Sarga, Dirk Wicke
and Mehmet Tekin
**Middle row,
from left**
Ania Wodzinska,
Melissa Rosenzweig
and Timothy Matney
**Front row,
from left**
Natalia
Kadzidłowska,
Barbara
Jakubowska,
Agnieszka
Poniewierska,
Kristina Sauer,
Judith Dosch,
Willis Monroe
and Kemalettin
Köroğlu

Introducing the team

The most important element of any scientific collaboration is the composition of the team. The right mix of disciplinary specialisations is the easy part, and most projects employ a combination of senior and junior scholars, professors and students; many, like ours, represent multiple, if not dozens, of nationalities. The real trick, though, is to find a group of people who work well together under the difficult conditions that we encounter in field archaeology: heat, dust and dirt, occasional lack of electricity and water, isolation from home, long hours and sometimes tedious jobs. Everyone has to do their tasks to ensure that the project works smoothly and they have to be willing to pitch in and help with jobs that benefit the whole project. At Ziyaret Tepe that meant we found zooarchaeologists and paleobotanists sweeping trenches before daybreak to make sure that the final photographs came out perfect. Archaeologists were frequently encountered counting and weighing pottery sherds when the ceramicists were overwhelmed with new materials. Even the director was seen wielding a shovel from time to time. It takes a team.

At Ziyaret Tepe, we had over 120 archaeologists and specialists working in the field with us during the course of our 18 field seasons. The senior staff was responsible for developing the overall research agenda, for fundraising and recruiting excavators and specialists. They were also principally responsible for publication, although many of our team participated in the writing of the reports, as they did in the production of this book. Over the years we developed a core team which remained relatively stable throughout long stretches of the project and provided continuity and training for new team members.

The beginning of the Ziyaret Tepe Archaeological Expedition was modest. For the first three seasons (1997–1999) the team was comprised of the project director, Prof. Timothy Matney (University of Akron, Ohio) and Prof. Guillermo Algaze (University of California, San Diego), who himself had led a number of expeditions and was an expert on pottery in the region, having conducted the only archaeological survey there in the 1980s.

Joining us in the early seasons were Eric Rupley, Dr Lewis Somers, a geophysicist from GeoScan Research USA, and later a geophysical survey team from the Middle East Technical Institute in Ankara.

The director,
Prof. Timothy Matney,
recalls:

Guillermo and I were finishing up a long-term joint project at the site of Titriş Höyük during these years, so the Ziyaret Tepe seasons were short – only a few weeks. Our goal was simple: to create a series of maps (topographic, surface pottery distribution and magnetic gradiometry) that would provide a general understanding of the periods of occupation at Ziyaret Tepe and serve as the basis for locating future excavations.

In 2000 we started excavation at the site based on the earlier survey results. At this time the size of the crew expanded to over a dozen people, and our first senior collaborators joined the Ziyaret Tepe Archaeological Expedition in 2000. Dr John MacGinnis (Cambridge University) took on the role of directing the archaeological operations in the lower town (Operation D), and Prof. Michael Roaf (University of Munich) started a project funded by the Deutsches Archäologisches Institut to cut a step-trench down the side of the high mound (Operation E) to establish a detailed chronology. Michael's project would last five seasons and would establish the formation of the site in the Early Bronze Age, roughly 3000 BC, and its nearly continuous occupation through to the end of the Neo-Assyrian period. A third excavation team under the direction of Duncan Schlee began the excavation of the Bronze Palace on the eastern edge of the citadel mound in 2000.

Field assistance was provided by a number of team members, some of whom returned for several seasons in this early period: Dr Andrew Bauer, Gülay Dinçkan, Dr David Dorren, Kaisa Akerman, Dr Adam Allentuck, Dr Diana Stein-Wuenscher, Peter Bartl, Çiğdem Maner, Dr Jeff Szuchman, Sara Kayser, Celine

Above
Prof. Dr Kemalettin Köroğlu at work in the dig-house

Above right
Professors Michael Roaf and Timothy Matney

Below
Judith Dosch excavates a drain

Right
Dr John MacGinnis defines a pit

Left
Prof. Michael
Roaf sweeps an
emerging
feature

Above
Frederike
Moll-Dau and
Mandy Reimann
clean a piece
of bitumen from
roof collapse

Top
Prof. Dr Dirk
Wicke at work
in the palace

Beauchamp and Dr Mary Shepperson. Two key members of our early house staff were Dr Paola Pugsley, our illustrator, and Helen McDonald, our ceramicist. Paola was the only team member to join me in all 15 excavation seasons and the corpus of her work is absolutely astounding – thousands of drawings which grace our preliminary reports, form a core of the archival database, and will play a vital role in the final analyses and publication series. In 2002 we were joined by epigrapher Prof. Simo Parpola, a leading expert on Neo-Assyrian texts, who translated the first cuneiform tablets found at Ziyaret Tepe.

In 2003 we were fortunate in recruiting a senior Turkish collaborator, Prof. Dr Kemalettin Köroğlu (Marmara University), who already had a long and impressive resumé of work in the Diyarbakır region. Kemalettin joined the team and began work on the excavations of the city's fortification walls in Operation K. His work over the next decade included several excavations in both the lower town and on the citadel. Kemalettin's expertise is the Iron Age of southeastern Turkey and he has written extensively on the Assyrians and their upland enemies, the Urartians. From the beginning, having a strong Turkish presence was important and we worked with a number of Turkish students and professionals throughout the project: Nurşen Fındık, Rıza Akgün, Zuhal Alcan, Mesut Alp, Harun Danışmaz, Burhan Süer and Armağan Tan.

By 2004 our team had grown to include around 30 foreign archaeologists and I made a number of changes to accommodate the needs of our expanded team. Most importantly, Dr Lynn Rainville, our microdebris specialist, was named assistant director to help the director in running day-to-day operations, and Lynn took over many of the tasks associated with the dig-house staff and specialists. We also recruited a young staff

member whose talents would change the project significantly. In 2004 Prof Dr Dirk Wicke (then of Johannes Gutenberg Universität Mainz) joined the Ziyaret Tepe Archaeological Expedition to continue his own research on ivory and ivory artefact production in the Assyrian period. In particular he worked on a deposit of burnt ivories found in a cremation burial in the Bronze Palace during the 2000–02 campaigns. In 2007 Dirk would return to excavate in the Bronze Palace with a team recruited from Mainz. His excavations there from 2007 to 2013 transformed our interpretation of that building.

After a study season in 2005, during which we expended considerable energy analysing and recording the finds from previous seasons, we resumed excavations in 2006 and continued without a break until the end of the field project in 2014. During this time the core senior staff was always present: Tim, John, Dirk and Kemalettin. Our digging crew included dozens of archaeologists over the years 2006–14 and again we were lucky to have a core of excavators who returned for multiple seasons: Judith Dosch, Kristina Sauer, Guido Schnell, Jennifer Walborn and Dominique Wiebe.

Although most people think that all archaeologists are diggers, the fact is that modern scientific expeditions have as many specialists as they do digging archaeologists. At Ziyaret Tepe, during our first seasons, the house staff was relatively limited. We had an illustrator, a ceramicist and one or two conservators, and Tim was responsible for the photography and the creation and maintenance of the project database.

Very quickly we expanded the number of specialists working at the site. We were fortunate to have a strong conservation staff who established a functioning professional field lab. Karen Abend, Mandy Reimann, Philipp Schmidt, Yvonne Helmholz, Charlotte Rerolle, Friederike

Above
Dr Mary
Shepperson taking
measurements in the
lower town

assisted by Marie Brondegaard Jensen. Even with these additions to the ceramics team, the sheer volume of pottery stored in the depot required more help, and in 2013 we were very fortunate to recruit Dr Ania Wodzinska, who brought with her a team of three very hard-working Polish undergraduate students who were able to complete the recording of a large backlog of material during the final two seasons. Another area of specialisation that required dedicated, long-term participation was the study of chipped stone, plant and animal remains.

Dr Britt Hartenberger, who had worked with Tim and Guillermo at Titriş Höyük, and in fact completed her doctoral dissertation on the chipped stone of the Early Bronze Age in southeastern Turkey, took on the job of, at first, describing and analysing chipped stone. She then added ground stone, and eventually also took over the processing and analysis of microdebris when Lynn left the project. Britt embodies the spirit of intellectual flexibility that makes a team work: whenever a job needs to be done, someone steps forward to help.

A number of zooarchaeological (animal bone) analysts have worked at Ziyaret Tepe: Dr Adam Allentuck, Dr Rémi Berthon and Dr Tina Greenfield. Tina joined the team in 2007 to collect her doctoral dissertation material and became a driving force in the reconstruction of the diet, economy and ecology of the region in the Neo-Assyrian period. In addition to her PhD dissertation, Tina has authored roughly a dozen papers and given a number of presentations on Ziyaret Tepe.

The following year, 2008, we recruited a young Chicago graduate student, Dr Melissa Rosenzweig, to analyse the paleobotanical (seed) remains from the Neo-Assyrian period for her doctoral dissertation. Teamed with Tina, Melissa's research has greatly increased our understanding of how the Assyrians at

Moll-Dau and Lourdes Mesa García all served for several years each, covering the basic field, laboratory and museum needs.

The geophysical surveys started by Dr Lewis Somers in 1998 continued and with the help of , and with the help of Ann Donkin, Jordan Bell and Chelsea Jalbrzikowski, undergraduates trained by Tim, ten seasons of magnetic gradiometry were completed. When our ceramicist Helen McDonald left the project, we recruited a number of specialists to help. It quickly became apparent that we would need a large ceramics crew, given the scale of our digging and intense ceramic analysis programme, and that we needed specialists in different periods. Azer Keskin took the lead in this project, returning to Ziyaret Tepe over a ten-year period and developing an internal site typology for the study of Assyrian pottery.

In 2011 we were joined by an expert in Islamic pottery, Dr Valentina Vezzoli, and in 2012 Dr Raffaella Papalardo added her expertise in the pottery of the Late Antique/Late Roman period, both ably

Tušhan ate, foddered their animals and used the ecosystems surrounding the settlement, including marshy areas near the Tigris River, the irrigation canals and the far-distant foothills of the Taurus Mountains. In 2013 Lucas Proctor joined Melissa in the paleobotanical lab to work on the Late Roman and Islamic seeds, and he is now expanding his interests and starting a doctoral dissertation on the Ziyaret Tepe plant remains.

The growing pains of the project from a few people to a team of 30 meant constantly finding and bringing new people onto the site. Several young scholars got their academic start at Ziyaret Tepe and contributed significantly to our intellectual progress. But the addition of more team members also meant an ever-expanding set of bureaucratic requirements: research visas, permits to excavate, permits to use government facilities for the dig-house, permits to close the trenches, requests to

export samples and to add materials to the museum inventories. Frequent trips to Diyarbakır to visit our accountant, pay our bills at the Mal Müdürlüğü (Revenue Department), collect residence permits and meet with museum representatives and so forth, meant that Tim had increasingly less time on site and a schedule often broken by trips.

Very quickly the tasks of photographer and registrar/data specialist were assumed by other team members. We had two excellent registrars who were able to piece together an intranet in the worst of all possible conditions: high heat, high dust and a variable, often non-existent, electrical supply. First Dr Birger Helgestad and then Dr Willis Monroe ably took charge and became the lynchpin of our database system, developing and adapting our recording procedures, creating protocols to ensure all finds coming in from the field were recorded and found

Left
Sometimes excavation continues back at the dig-house. Jennifer Walborn (left) and Chelsea Jalbrzikowski (right) sieve the earth taken from a burial to look for very small bones that may have been missed during excavation

their way to the appropriate specialist.

We also found a number of excellent photographers who were able to assist us and whose images form the vast bulk of the illustrations in this volume: Jerzy Wierzbicki, Simo Rista, Ian J. Cohn and Hilary McDonald. As described in the section on photography, this is an extremely important and challenging position, a mixture of art and science. Much of the work was highly repetitive – for example, taking standardised photographs of small metal studs which were found by the hundred but needed to be recorded nonetheless – and tested the patience of all our photographers, but as the illustrations here show, the results were worth the effort.

The team also included many other people who came to Ziyaret Tepe, including visiting specialists and students. The list is very long indeed. Of course, there is another vital component to the team that must be mentioned, and that is the recruitment of workmen. Each year, the mayor of Tepe presented me with a list of workmen looking for employment and requested politely that we employ as many as possible. Some were the mayor's kinsmen, some were his friends, others were villagers who really needed money or had fallen on difficult times. This discussion was always a negotiation, as our needs and budget rarely matched the lengthy list that the mayor had developed.

We usually hired around 50–70 workmen. One season we had over 100 on the payroll, but found that this number was too large to manage effectively. We hired a foreman (çavuş) whose job was to ensure that the workmen were at the site on time (which meant arriving in the dark), ready to work, and that any issues or problems such as illnesses and family disputes were settled with minimum impact on the archaeological work in the trench.

We had two excellent, responsible foremen at Ziyaret Tepe – İbrahim Sun and Süleyman Altun – who greatly facilitated our work. We also hired a local site guard whose job it was to sleep on the high mound, overlooking the excavation areas and tools. At the house we usually employed two or three women from the village to help with washing pottery and animal bones, and with general housekeeping at the camp.

A famous quote says that 'an army marches on its stomach' and hungry archaeologists are no different. Perhaps the most important job was that of the cook and we had one of the finest field cooks in Turkey, Necmi Yaşar, who prepared food and drink on what was often no more than a glorified camp stove, collected supplies from various village businesses, and co-ordinated many of the behind-the-scenes activities at the dig-house to ensure that the archaeologists didn't have to worry about much except archaeology. Necmi worked with Guillermo and me at Titriş Höyük and was indispensable for the smooth functioning of the house and keeping the army marching forward.

The other key position was the driver and we had two excellent drivers at Ziyaret Tepe: Mustafa Kılıçal, who like Necmi was a veteran of the Titriş Höyük campaigns, and, after his retirement, Mehmet Tekin. A driver does far more than just drive the dig vehicle, and Mehmet could be seen doing everything from shopping to setting up security fences, and on more than one occasion collecting geophysical survey data! He worked from sunup to sundown with indefatigable energy. Once we had secured Necmi's and Mehmet's services for a season we could rest assured that the basic logistics were covered.

Finally, all of the work was overseen by a government representative (temsilci), appointed by the Ministry of Culture in Ankara: we were fortunate to work with a collection of helpful representatives over our 18-year project.

59

Overleaf
A timeless scene as sheep, goats and shepherd head for the pastures at dawn

A day in the life of the dig director

My alarm rings at 3.30am. The camp is dark and quiet. The breeze coming in through the window of my room is as cool as I am going to feel all day. The shower is cold water, at least most seasons, since the compound that we rent from the government doesn't have functioning hot water. Ice-cold water is in any case just fine by me. After all, one of the constants of working in Diyarbakır Province in the summer is the heat. Endless weeks of temperatures hovering around 40°C with no clouds and no rain make the cold water an appealing respite. I'm instantly awake and in my head running through a list of things to be done.

First breakfast for the field team starts at 4am: tea, coffee, biscuits. Necmi has been up as long as I have, getting water and supplies ready for the field team. By convention, the house staff – the conservators, ceramicists, illustrator, photographer and other specialists – will get up around 5.30am and have their first breakfast, then settle into work as soon as there is enough light coming through the windows.

Shortly before 4.30am Mehmet arrives and the field team packs all the equipment they need for the day into the van. The dig-house is in the village of Tepe and the ancient

Clockwise from left Mehmet with his van; Murat's horse and cart; Prof. Köroğlu draws a section; team breakfast on site

site lies a few kilometres east of the village. Although the distance isn't far, the roads are uneven at best and often filled with livestock headed to pasture, so the drive takes about 15 minutes. Piles of technical equipment such as an electronic 'total station', dumpy levels, drawing frames and cameras sit beside empty metal buckets and rubber zembils awaiting the day's finds, dig-bags crammed with notebooks, pens, tags and the most delicate digging tools, small dental picks and brushes. The heavy tools are left on site,

where we employ a site guard who spends the night on a makeshift sleeping platform watching over the excavation areas and making sure our dig equipment is safe. We are lucky. We have a good relationship with the villagers in the region and never have any serious problems with theft or looting.

The van is generally silent as we bump our way across the rutted roads and drop team members off at their various excavation areas. Typically, we will excavate in three or four

Above Sunrise on site in the cool early morning
Below İbrahim, our foreman (right), oversees workmen and offers advice

different locations. Each dig area is directed by a senior archaeologist, and several assistants who are sometimes the graduate students of the area director, or other archaeologists recruited to the project, to help with the digging.

As scientific director my job is to co-ordinate all the activities with the area directors – setting out strategies and goals, thinking about the big picture – and to make sure all the teams have the resources they need.

Over the course of the morning I will walk between the excavation areas and discuss the details of the day's work with the staff, offer ideas on digging tactics, and help with any logistical problems. John needs more workmen for the morning – can anyone spare a few? Is it a good

idea to expand our excavation area, or to continue to excavate to a greater depth? Most importantly, I get to discuss in great detail what was found the day before and to participate in the evolution of our interpretation of the site.

For me, this is the best part of the day. Months of planning and preparation, endless paperwork, fundraising and emails, have all led to this: a crisp summer morning overlooking the Tigris River Valley, the sun just creeping up over the horizon, the air clear and the only noise the industrious scraping and brushing of the workmen, punctuated by a squeaky wheelbarrow moving dirt to the spoil heap.

Our foreman calls the roll to make sure all the workmen are here on time. The focus of the team is intense. Everyone has a job – well, several jobs – to do and while most of the work is pretty mundane – writing tags, sweeping away dirt from a room under excavation, making drawings and taking photographs – it is immensely satisfying. Slowly we are seeing the appearance of individual lines of the mud bricks, then walls and floors, then the plan of whole buildings emerging from the earth, and with this a

Overleaf
A busy morning in Operation M

Above
Dr Paola Pugsley draws features on site

Right, top Prof. Matney explains the progress of the excavation to the foreman, Süleyman Altun

hardboiled eggs, and hot tea.

We all meet under a common breakfast shade and there is usually a great deal of chatter as people discuss the morning's work, talk logistics and relax for half an hour. The workmen break into

smaller groups and sit under their own shades, eating breakfasts they have brought. They might send one of the younger fellows down to a local field to bring back a watermelon for them to share.

The foreman's whistle calls us back to work. The field crew will continue to dig until 12.30pm, when we generally break for lunch. In the trenches the late morning presents a different set of working conditions. The heat is distracting and energy-draining; team members drink litres of water to

keep hydrated and it is hard to stay focused.

As the sun gets higher in the sky, the colours of the soil turn a uniform grey-brown and it becomes harder to dig effectively. Because the areas we are digging are so large (our typical trench is 10 x 10m and we may be digging in as many as four trenches simultaneously in one area), it is impossible to put shades over the excavations. The staff and workmen are in the direct sun all day. There is a physicality to field archaeology that shouldn't be

picture of life at the site in ancient times. In some ways the project is like working on a giant jigsaw puzzle, with a lot of missing pieces.

Around 8.30am the van arrives with second breakfast from the dig-house. Necmi prepares a full breakfast for us and by this time of the morning everyone is hungry. It isn't hot yet – usually around 30°C – but we all know that the heat is coming. Breakfast is a real feast: fresh, hot local flatbread, honey, cheese, tomatoes, cucumbers, watermelon, olives, scrambled and

Clockwise from above
Goats traverse the mound; Mustafa takes a well-earned rest; food by Necmi; relaxing under the canopy at the house

exhaustion are a good combination for a refreshing nap. Some of the staff will walk into town to visit the internet café, others will just relax and read a novel. Tea is served at 3.30pm, along with biscuits, and if we're lucky Necmi will bring out a cake dripping with honey, fresh from the oven.

Work starts again at 4pm. The field crew will often head back into the field to finish drawings and notes, work on problem excavation areas, and plan out the next day's work without the need for constantly supervising the workmen.

Of course, there is never a shortage of work back at the dig-house: photographs need to be labelled and filed, field notes completed, updates made to the online database, weekly

underestimated. The team will work eight-hour days, six days a week, for eight or nine weeks, so stamina is important. We have a saying in the field. 'All decisions made after 11am are wrong!' While not strictly true, by the end of eight hours in the sun it is easy to make mistakes: mislabel tags, confuse stratigraphy.

By 12.30pm the excavators are hot, dusty and tired. Their last task is to take photographs documenting the day's digging, and to ensure that all the buckets of pottery, bones and stone artefacts are labelled and loaded into the car for transporting to the dig-house.

A full lunch is served in the dig-house at 1.30pm, after which there is a time to relax. On most days there is business for me in

Diyarbakır – residence permits, museum paperwork, meetings with our accountant, shopping – so Mehmet and I take off for the big city directly after lunch. On the weekends, when all the offices are closed, I enjoy a nap for an hour or so. The dig-house is hot, but as long as we have electricity and can run the ubiquitous fans that are found in every room, the moving air and

100

summaries written. The house staff includes a number of specialists and the excavators from time to time will be called on to help them with processing pottery, or to consult about finds from a previous day, or to advise the photographer and illustrator.

As the sun starts to set shortly before 7pm, the field crew wraps up work on site just as the mosquitoes rise and the daylight fades. At the end of each working day, the entire team joins together for an informal 'happy hour', when we relax over a cold beer, fruit juice or a gin and tonic (when we can find tonic water and limes!) and snacks of pistachios and hazelnuts. As happy-hour attendance is required, it is the perfect

Clockwise from top left
Small picks advance in line; the minibus packed up for return to the dig-house; tea (*çay*) in the village; varying forms of transport to and from the dig, with Ziyaret Tepe in the background

time to chat, talk about the news of the day, gossip about our workmen (as they do at the tea houses about us) and plot tomorrow's work. Keeping a team of 25 archaeologists happy and working well together means making sure that everyone socialises at least a bit and feels a part of the team. Our happy hour is

an enjoyable chance to really get to know our fellows. We often hold it outside, under the early night sky.

Sometime around 7.45pm, Necmi will call *'Yemek!'* (food) and the team migrates quickly to the dinner table for a final meal. By 9pm most people have started wandering towards their beds, although there are always a few team members who stay up and enjoy the quiet personal time that is so rare in the cramped working conditions of the dig-house.

The field team makes sure all their equipment is charged and dig-bags packed, ready to go in the morning. By 10pm most are sound asleep under mosquito nets, whirring fans stirring the still-warm air, the silence punctuated by the occasional dog barking in the village.

Geophysics

When archaeologists work at a place as large as Ziyaret Tepe, it is impossible to excavate all, or even most, of the site. Instead we need to learn as much as possible about what might be below ground before starting to dig. Typically archaeologists do this in two ways. First we assess what is on the modern surface of the ground by collecting artefacts and plotting their spatial distributions. In 1997 we completed a systematic survey of the surface of Ziyaret Tepe, determining the periods when people lived on the site and where they were active. For example, we found considerable numbers of Roman pottery

sherds and roof tiles in the lower town, but none from the *höyük*, suggesting that Roman occupation was limited to the lower portions of the site.

The second means by which archaeologists assess what is below ground before excavating is through a suite of technologies known collectively as archaeological geophysics. Broadly, geophysical prospection attempts to map underground or subsurface features such as walls, pits and floors by measuring a physical property of the earth. Three techniques were used at Ziyaret Tepe to map the ancient city: magnetic gradiometry, electrical resistivity and ground-penetrating radar. In all, we conducted ten seasons of geophysical survey and mapped the entire lower town with at least one technique.

Magnetic gradiometry measures minute fluctuations in the strength and direction of the earth's magnetic field caused by underground features. A buried piece of iron, for instance, is highly magnetic and its individual magnetic field, although tiny compared to that of the earth itself, is sufficiently strong to be mapped with a gradiometer. With this technique we were able to map fired installations like kilns, as well as some of the larger mud-brick walls used in monumental architecture. A handheld magnetometer was passed over the earth following a strict grid pattern and the resulting maps show fluctuations in the magnetic field. These maps were then used to predict the location of

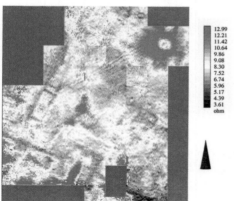

well-preserved architecture. With this technique we were able to map a number of features in the lower town, including the large public building in Operation G.

Electrical resistivity is an active survey technique, meaning that our instruments put energy into the ground (in this case in the form of an electrical current) and then measure how subsurface features interfere with the propagation of that energy. In the case of electrical resistivity what we are measuring is the ease with which an electrical current can pass through a volume of soil. Certain conditions, like soil moisture and salinity, affect the current by allowing a greater flow of electrical current, while other features, such as large stones or highly compact surfaces, create greater resistance. A handheld electrical resistance meter mounted on a frame with two or more iron probes is inserted into the ground for each datapoint taken, so this is a slow technique. In the case of Ziyaret Tepe, though, the effort was worthwhile, as we were able to map both high- and low-resistance features with considerable clarity. This provided a map of the southern city gate, the fortification walls and towers, an open courtyard, and a series of storage rooms ultimately excavated as Operations K, Q and V.

The working conditions at Ziyaret Tepe were not ideal for geophysical survey. The tall stubble from the harvested wheat was difficult to walk through with our

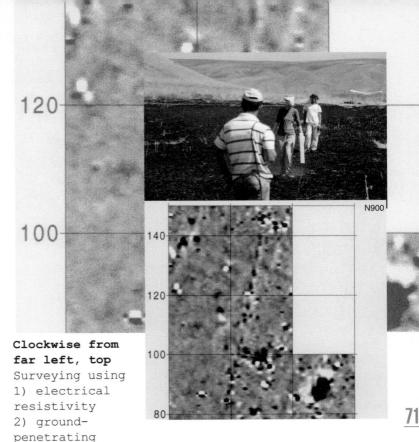

N900

71

Clockwise from far left, top
Surveying using 1) electrical resistivity 2) ground-penetrating radar 3) magnetic gradiometry; burning the stubble from a field; electrical resistivity map of Assyrian remains in the lower town

instruments, prompting us occasionally to burn off the fields to allow our surveyor to walk without hindrance. Likewise, the scorching summer sun meant that there was little soil moisture near the surface, so we had laboriously to add water to the ground in order to be able to generate an electrical field. Still, the results allowed us to target specific areas for excavation with great savings in terms of time and effort.

Registration of the finds

Much like objects in a museum, archaeological finds are recorded in great detail. It is the job of the registrar to keep everything carefully organised and to describe all of the objects coming in from the field. This work primarily takes place in the offices of the dig-house rather than out on site, but for large objects or special finds registration might take place in the field as well.

The job begins before the digging even starts with the design of a database for the project, and the organisational structure for how objects will move around the dig offices, allowing the diverse group of researchers to conduct their analyses. Every step and study of the objects needs to be accounted for in the database so that an accurate location of every object is maintained.

Every object, bucket of pottery, bag of bones or sample of soil gets its own unique identification number for the site (more than 48,000 by the end of the project). In addition, every entry needs a 'find spot', either the locus (context) in which it was found or even the precise location measured by total station, the electronic instrument used for surveying. The precise recording of find spots is critical to the scientific analysis of the excavated materials. Once objects have been given a number and a location, the registrar spends time describing the object in detail, taking measurements and noting important features. All of this information gets entered into the database and serves as a first record of the object. From there the objects proceed to different places

Above Buckets of pottery brought in from the field

Right Crates of ceramics waiting for processing

around the dig-house, depending on their conservation status and importance to specific researchers. Everything gets photographed and these photos are also stored in the database. By the end of a season the project has an account of everything that was excavated from the site recorded in detail.

Above
Willis Monroe's cat finds a comfortable place to sleep by the database at the registration desk

Left
Britt Hartenberger standing amidst crates of ground stone artefacts awaiting her attention

Below
The copious excavation files; tagged bone finds

Above
Willis Monroe, the registrar, ready for duty

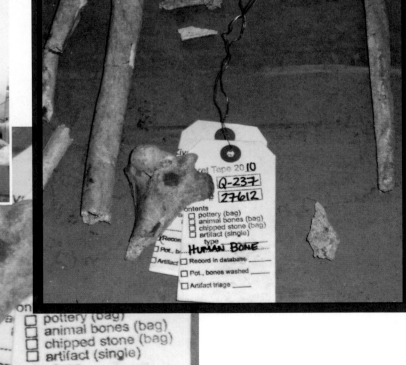

pottery (bag)
animal bones (bag)
chipped stone (bag)
artifact (single)
type
HUMAN BONE

Record in database

Drawing at Tepe

Illustrator Paola Pugsley

A picture, as they say, is worth a thousand words. In archaeology that is truly so when the picture is a drawing. Not unlike a fashion photographer and a top model, a drawing brings out the 'best profile', mutes blemishes, glosses over casual breakages. enhancing all important features. Drawing also means getting to know the object and handling it, occasionally wearing gloves (awkward, but it keeps the conservators happy). This is the draughtsperson's main perk, which is probably what attracted me to the job and kept me to my drawing table for 15 summers.

Drawing at Tepe made for an itinerant lifestyle. Daylight is best – in the early morning when it is nippy – and direct sunlight is a blessing, but after 10am you want the shade. In the afternoon, after siesta time, you have to move again.

With the table comes the necessary complement of tools – calipers, dividers, Blu Tack, set squares, pencils, eraser and odds and ends that have proved useful at some point and that you want to hang on to just in case. Last but not least the iPod. Music is mainly classical, with some contemporary input from my children. And the complete works of Shakespeare, which I had never tackled before.

Sometimes work is on site for those 'small finds' that are not exactly small, like the huge pithoi storage jars that sometimes do not travel very well. It makes for a welcome change of routine and, if properly timed, for second breakfast on top of the mound with a full view of the Tigris below.

Where do all these works of art go? Most will end up in the archive, the all-important translation of the excavation process onto paper that will enable people to reconstruct it; some will see daylight in publications complementing text. Occasionally some finds, such as the little monkey sniffing a flower, enjoy a new lease of life on the dig's T-shirts, albeit after some topical adjustments.

Above and left
Dr Paola Pugsley, our peerless illustrator

Above right
Iron scale armour from Operation L

Below right
Bronze omphalos bowl from the Achaemenid grave in Operation G

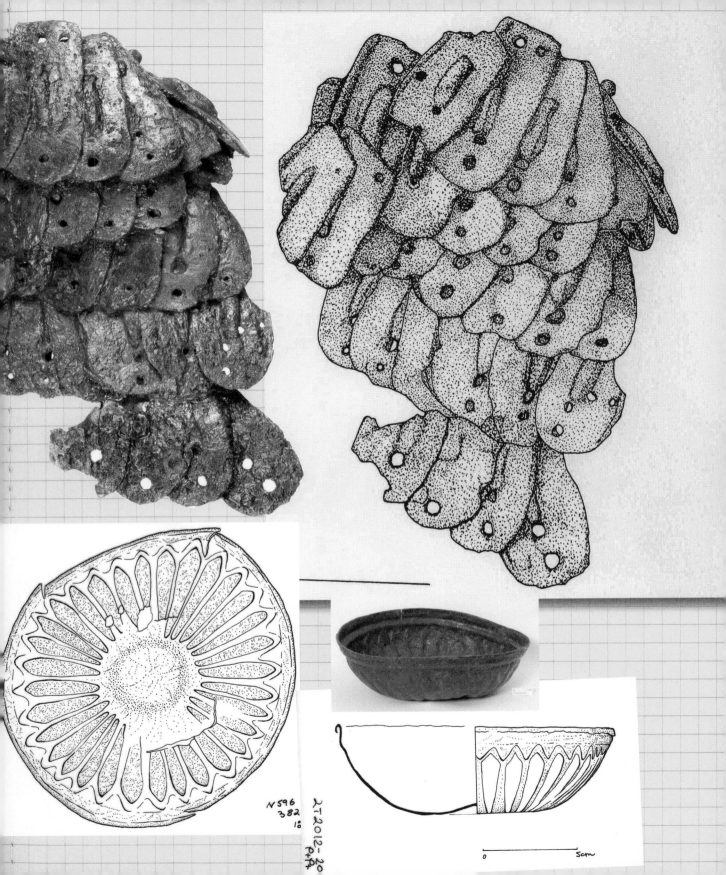

N596
382
10

2T2012-20
PP

An artist
in residence

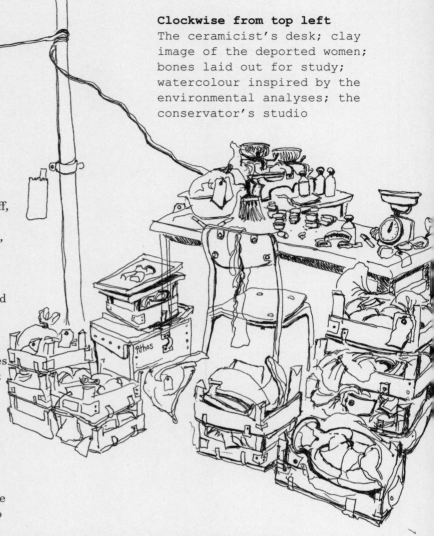

Clockwise from top left
The ceramicist's desk; clay image of the deported women; bones laid out for study; watercolour inspired by the environmental analyses; the conservator's studio

In the 2014 season we were joined by a new member of staff, Alex Hirtzel, who came in the role of artist in residence. Alex, who had previously worked on archaeological projects in Jordan, fitted into the team seamlessly. While the specialists worked on their classifying and scientific analyses of the finds from the excavation, Alex approached these materials from a different angle. During her time with us in Turkey she drew bones laid out for sorting and potsherds laid out for dating; gathered images of the conservator's table; peered through a microscope at the dust and seed particles scraped from the throne-room floor; admired the impressive piles of the non-diagnostic ceramic potsherds. Alex drew with pen and ink all day.

Back in her studio in the UK, from these drawings she has retold stories, picked up references, and reordered them from the mythical age of thousands of years ago into a new narrative of her own. She mostly made layered prints and objects in clay. In her exhibitions these have been laid out as installations – in a domestic cabinet of curiosities, in a suitcase, on a trestle table, in a chest of drawers. She has made ceramic caskets, memorials (like so many broken potsherds repaired through time) to the lost, unspoken many who once lived at Ziyaret Tepe and worked to make it the bustling place it was. For instance, from the cuneiform clay tablet (see page 96) listing the names of 144 women, Alex has retold their story – an amazing tale, imagined in clay.

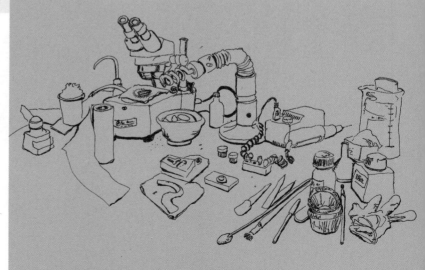

'They stand on the shore, waiting for the sign to tell them it is time, time to step into the boat, with their children, to take them to their new life. They wait to see what will become of them, uprooted and frightened. They are now under the authority of another administration. The list states their name and the village they are assigned to, or whether they are "at the disposal of" named supervisors'

Left
Alex Hirtzel put on a mini-exhibition in the dig-house for the archaeologists, followed by more formal exhibitions in London and Cambridge

Below and Right
Caskets inspired by tales of Assyrian gods and stories relating to ancient Tušhan

Photography on site

One of the most important records made at any archaeological excavation is the photographic record. The Ziyaret Tepe photographic archive comprises over 120,000 images taken during our expedition. When we first started work in 1997, digital photography was in its infancy. Available digital cameras were expensive, awkward and produced poor-quality images that were not suitable for publication. We used three film cameras – one for colour slides, used for presentations; one for black-and-white prints used for publications; and one for colour-print film which provided colour images required for the museum records. Cameras, 50-plus rolls of film and a variety of lenses, filters, bellows for macroscopic photography, studio lights and tripods were a considerable investment of funds and luggage space.

It was not possible to get slide or black-and-white film processed in Diyarbakır with any hope of decent quality, so we carefully labelled each roll of film and listed each each image in a photographic logbook. Heat, dust, exposure to security X-rays at airports and the possibility of losing all the film during travel made photography a very challenging part of the early expedition.

The relief when we got back to the US and received the film and contact prints for the black-and-white images showing that we had usable images was tremendous. Given those constraints, the early campaigns produced fewer than

2,000 images each. Our first digital camera, the Mavica, used 3.5in floppy disks as 'film' and recorded six low-resolution images on a single disk. While the images were not suitable for publication, they did provide a back-up in case the film cameras failed.

There were basically two kinds of photographs that we took on site: artefact records and field records. Once good digital cameras were available we took photographs of every artefact uncovered on the expedition (except pottery sherds, bones and pieces of chipped stone, which together numbered several million pieces). These basic record shots were meant for research purposes only, so the goal was to record as many angles as needed with good lighting and a scale. We uploaded a thumbnail of each image into our electronic database and stored the high-resolution versions for later use. A selection of artefacts that were going to be given to the Diyarbakır Museum or that we knew were going to be published were given special treatment with additional views and greater care over lighting. About 4,200 small finds were registered in this way, meaning this laborious task was the

Clockwise from top left Digging a pit; indigenous Iron Age 'grooved ware' pottery; Jerzy Wierzbicki gets a bird's-eye view; a handy pit for discussions; kite view of Operation R: a section of mosaic can just be made out

principal job of the photographer. We were fortunate at Ziyaret Tepe to work with four professional photographers over the course of the project: Hilary McDonald, Ian J. Cohn, Jerzy Wierzbicki and Simo Rista, whose excellent photographs are found throughout this book.

Photographing the progress of work in the field required considerable ingenuity. As any photographer knows, the key to making strong photographic images is light. In the photographic studio back at the dig-house we could control the light quite easily by darkening the windows with a curtain and using artificial lights. Mirrors or white reflective cards, placed strategically, allowed us to produce very good-quality lighting. In the field the photographers were at the mercy of the relentless Turkish sun. Photographs taken after the sun was very far above the horizon suffered badly from the harsh lighting, which washed out colours or created deep, dark shadows. The dust accumulated over the course of a working day further obscured our subjects. In archaeological photography, the contrast between soil colours is both vitally important and subtle, so the noonday sun is terrible for taking on-site photographs.

Much of the work of photographing took place at first light, or occasionally at dusk, when the sun, low on the horizon, provided perfect light for photography. The problem was that as soon as the sun rose above the horizon, the edges of our trenches produced sharp shadows that obscured the architecture we were photographing.

One trick we used was to stretch large pieces of clear plastic behind the photographer, held aloft by workmen employing wooden poles. The plastic sheeting served to diffuse the light, breaking up the shadows and creating a gentle light that showed the contrasting soil colours and subtle archaeological features well. Of course, we still only

Clockwise from far left Suphi Kaya sorts microdebris from a sieve; artefacts in crates awaiting processing (the coloured tag system helped us prioritise our recording work); tools at the ready; the photographer's studio
Following pages Excavations under way in the Bronze Palace; early-morning cleaning in Operation L; the lowest levels of the palace

had a few minutes to photograph, since the sun quickly rose over the top of our plastic sheeting.

Many of our photographs were meant to cover large areas, even entire excavation areas, so our photographers often found themselves high up on ladders. We even experimented with flying our cameras on kites with an electronic remote control to advance the film. These were the days before drones, so our kite system was handmade. Because of security concerns in the Diyarbakır area, we were not allowed to employ either balloons (which have the advantage of flying on totally windless days, unlike kites) or low-flying aircraft, such as crop dusters, until the final season of excavation, when a Turkish team came and took photographs using a balloon system.

The areas of excavation were swept meticulously before photographing, which meant that on occasion we would have very early morning parties in which the entire team – house staff and field crew

alike – would come out well before sunrise to spend an hour or so sweeping all the accumulated dust and dirt out of an area before those few precious minutes when the photographer would be able to take the necessary shots. The final results speak for themselves.

This page
Not every
problem had
an easy
solution!

Right Members
of the team
work on
processing
ceramics in the
afternoon

Chapter 3
Work on the Tušhan excavations begins

The preceding chapters explored the landscape of the upper Tigris valley, the background against which the Ziyaret Tepe Archaeological Expedition came into being, and the day-to-day functioning of operations. We turn now to the excavations themselves and the many wonderful things they uncovered.

Above The palace of the governor emerges from its clayey matrix

The royal palace

'A royal palace for my kingship I had constructed at Tušhan' – thus spake Ashurnasirpal II according to his famous stele inscription, the Kurkh Monolith, referring to the palace he constructed at Ziyaret Tepe. We believe this is the building we excavated on the high mound and dubbed the Bronze Palace. Massive remains of mud-brick structures on the eastern edge of the mound had drawn our attention to this spot, and this is where in 2000 the excavations at Ziyaret Tepe were inaugurated. Operations were then carried out in 2000–2002 and 2007–2014. Despite this, only a small part of the plan was exposed. For one thing, a significant part of the building had already been eroded down the slope, in addition to which there is heavy pitting from the Hellenistic, Roman and medieval periods. On top of that, the poor preservation of the mud brick – in places in any case only preserved one course thick – made it very difficult to follow, requiring very careful excavation. Nevertheless, by the end we were able to uncover the central suite of the palace, part of the domestic wing and half of its associated courtyard.

The plan of the building appears to follow the standard layout of Assyrian palaces, with a central reception room situated between an outer, public courtyard (the *babānu*) and an inner, private courtyard (the *bitānu*). The reception room was equipped with limestone trackways for a mobile hearth to be moved up and down the room to keep it warm in wintertime. It was decorated with colourful painted wall-

plaster, whose designs of crenellations, concentric circles and palmettes in blue, red and orange outlined in black against a white background closely resemble the decoration of royal palaces in the capital cities of Nineveh and Nimrud. Effectively, this made the palace at Tušhan a true 'royal palace', even though the king would only have actually resided there on the relatively few occasions when he passed through in the course of military campaigns.

The reception room had direct access to a washroom behind. This and the other palace bathrooms were tiled with baked bricks set in bitumen for waterproofing, all serviced by an elaborate array of drains and cesspits beneath the floors.

The palace was kept scrupulously clean, with only a few finds left behind for archaeologists to discover. The most important was unquestionably the cuneiform tablet ZTT 30 – a list of women in the employ of the palace who appear to have been deported from far away. Otherwise we mostly found pottery, including, appropriately, the finely crafted, very thin tableware known as 'palace ware'.

The most spectacular find was the discovery in the courtyard of the cremation burials, still intact and with a large number of grave goods. A deep sounding carried out in order to investigate earlier phases revealed remains of a previous palace dating to the Middle Assyrian period, very likely constructed when the Assyrians first arrived in the upper Tigris region and a colony was founded at Tušhan. This building must have fallen into ruins by the time Ashurnasirpal II returned to the site and had a massive mud-brick platform laid as foundation for his palace. The Neo-Assyrian palace appears to have undergone at least one rebuilding, probably during the mid-to-late 8th century BC, when some of the rooms, including the reception room, were enlarged. The building itself does not

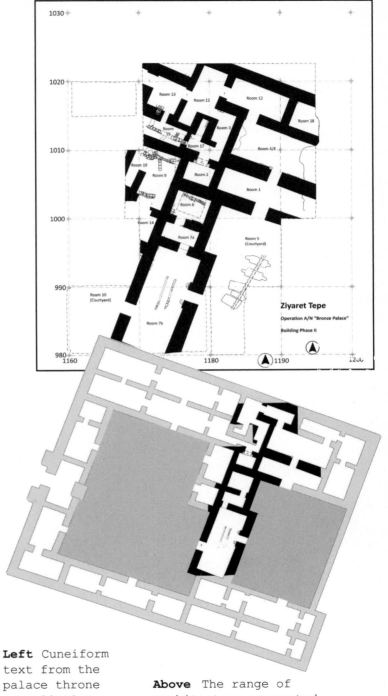

Left Cuneiform text from the palace throne room listing women whose names appear to belong to a previously unknown language

Above The range of architecture excavated in Operation A/N, with a reconstruction of its place in the overall layout of the palace

show any traces of destruction but was probably just left open to the elements when the last Assyrian governor vacated the city before the advance of the Babylonian army in 611 BC. The massive walls were subsequently used for a later (squatter) occupation, but once that too ended, the site was abandoned and memory of its great days faded into the mists of time.

Left, top to bottom
The throne-room suite; a cuneiform tablet after being removed from the ground; wall plaster undergoing conservation

Right
The decorated wall plaster fully conserved, ready for display in the museum in Diyarbakır

Above
Palace-ware vessels from the palace

Mud brick: unsung star of the archaeologist's world

Mud brick was invented in the Neolithic period, nine thousand years ago, and proved to be one of the great inventions of mankind. Mud bricks are made by mixing mud or clay with water, adding straw, pebbles and other inclusions such as broken pottery for strength. The mixture is then poured into brick moulds and left to dry in the sun. Although in many countries it has given way to baked brick and other materials, mud brick is a marvellous medium, wonderfully organic and malleable, environmentally friendly and very suited to fluctuations in temperature.

Of course one disadvantage of mud brick is that it is susceptible to erosion by water: to counter this, walls need to be regularly replastered and cracks in roofs rolled out. For rooms with a high water use – kitchens and bathrooms – the floors and

Above Mud brickwork of the palace from above

Right A close-up of one of the monumental walls

sides could be tiled with baked bricks. But the wood needed as fuel for this made it very expensive and as a result such features are markers of elite buildings, whether temples, palaces or high-status residences (though these bricks were often subsequently reused in non-elite contexts).

For archaeologists another great advantage is that the dimensions of the bricks change over the ages and can as a consequence be used as a tool for dating. In antiquity – and even today – bricks could also be stamped with an inscription telling us who commissioned the building and perhaps what type of building it was and what city it was in. This could be done on both baked and unbaked bricks. Sadly none of the bricks at Ziyaret Tepe were inscribed – and we checked a lot of bricks!

In the village there are still some mud-brick houses, though these have more and more been replaced by modern concrete structures, including the team's own quarters. Although these have, of course, many advantages, they lose out to mud brick in one respect: they are hot in the summer and cold in the winter.

Top Left
Puddling clay for making mud bricks in a pit close to the village

Left
Mud-brick houses in the village

Above
Mud bricks laid
out to dry and
stacked
awaiting use

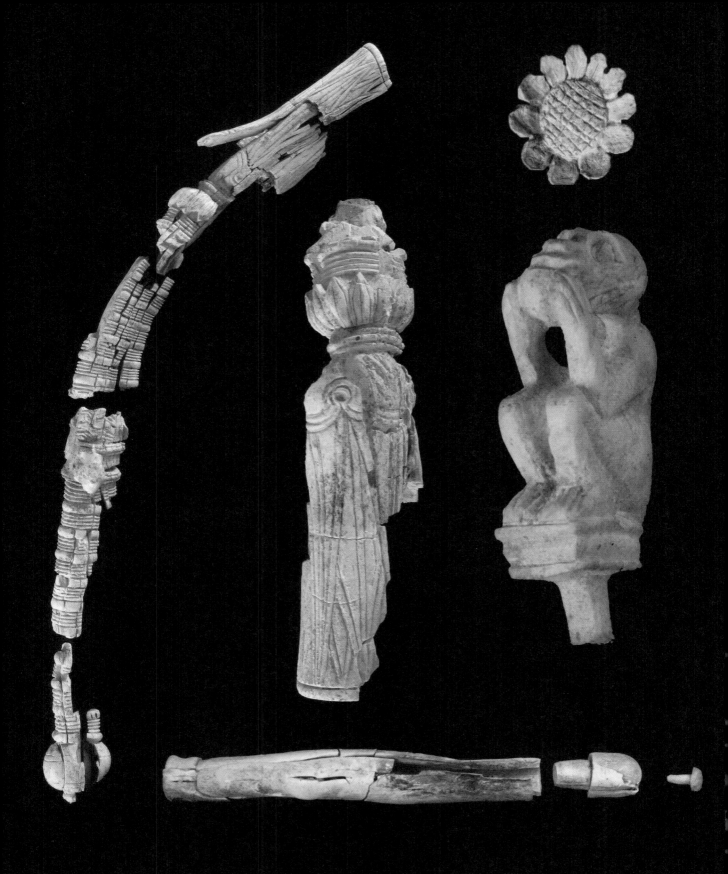

The palace cremation burials

Some of the most unusual and most unexpected finds from the palace were made in the very first season of excavating. These were rectangular pits lined with a thin layer of scorched soil measuring in the order of 2 x 1.4m, some with shallow protrusions at the narrow ends. In the heavy ash fill which they contained, a large number of bronze objects were discovered, which ultimately gave the name to the edifice – the Bronze Palace. The pieces included shallow bowls and smaller containers, a lamp and a quantity of thin strips. The bronzes were in a very poor state of preservation, mostly rather fragmented, heavily corroded and distorted by heat. It became clear these pieces must have been burnt in situ in the pits and left to be buried in the ashes.

The meaning of these depositions was at first a mystery, since at first glance the pits looked like bronze-working installations, though the location, inside a palace, was definitely not a place for a smithy. A number of similarly heavily burnt clay vessels and ivory pieces were found with them in the ashes. Since ivory does not burn, but rather blackens, discolours and warps, it is a good indicator for the burning temperature. Comparative studies established that the temperature in these pits must have reached well above 1100°C, explaining the state of preservation of the bronzes which, judging from the formation of droplets on some pieces, had reached melting point.

It was only in 2007 and 2008, with the

Above
A cremation burial in the course of excavation

Left
Ivories recovered from the cremation burials

discovery of two further pits containing severely burnt human bones, that these features were correctly identified as primary cremation burials. Roughly comparable to the Roman *bustum* type of burial, a cremation burial is a form of interment in which a pit is dug into the ground, wood laid down to form a pyre, the body of the deceased placed onto this, together with grave goods, and the whole ensemble burnt in situ. Instead of separating the bones from the ashes and collecting them into an urn, the cremated human remains and the associated funerary gifts are left in place. In order to facilitate ventilation for the cremation, flues can be included at the narrow ends of the grave-pit, as was the case with three of the cremation burials in the palace at Ziyaret Tepe. High temperatures are needed to fully cremate the body, and this explains the poor preservation of the bronzes, ivories and other objects.

In all, five cremation burials were discovered in the palace, neatly located right under the paved courtyard, each one containing the remains of one individual. Although the cremation process itself must have smoked the place out, the location of the burials within the living quarters of the palace conforms with the Mesopotamian practice of burying the dead in domestic areas in order to keep contact with the family. A similar situation was discovered at the site of Tell Sheikh Hamad on the river Khabur in Syria, where cremation burials were found even inside rooms, the rooms subsequently being refitted and replastered after the burning to make them habitable again. The burials were accompanied by rich goods indicating the high status of the deceased, who were most likely part of the governor's household, perhaps even the governor himself.

The practice of cremation is, however, very unusual, since according to Assyrian belief burning equates with the destruction of the body, leaving the soul of the dead in the netherworld with no identity. Cremation burials, especially in their more common form where the bones are interred in an urn, are thus very rare in Assyria proper, although more widely distributed in the Levant, northeastern Syria and Eastern Anatolia.

The discovery of this kind of burial at sites such as Tell Sheikh Hamad and Ziyaret Tepe suggests there was a change in Assyrian belief and burial customs. Or, to put it another way, this is a textbook example of cultural hybridisation, with the ruling elite of Tušhan blending Assyrian and non-Assyrian practices in their funerary rites. This may in turn suggest that at least some of the ruling class were of non-Assyrian origin, something also suggested by the fact that the names of some of the governors of Tušhan also betray a non-Assyrian background.

Above Ceramic offerings emerge

Left A typical Assyrian drinking goblet

Right Bronze juglet with riveted handle and engraving

Burial practices

For the Assyrians, life continued after death in the netherworld in the form of spirits who wanted to take part in daily life and needed to receive food and drink from the living. The dead were considered still to be part of the family and were frequently buried inside their houses, beneath the floors. According to Assyrian belief, the grave was the door into the underworld and the place for ancestral worship. It was usual to equip the deceased with offerings of food and drinks, together with personal items, in order to provide nourishment for the journey into the underworld and for future use once there.

The Assyrians practised various forms of burial, mostly depending on the economic status of the individual families. Rich families would generally construct burial vaults, most often a single chamber with a vertical shaft leading down from the surface. The dead were laid out on their backs, wrapped in shrouds, surrounded by gifts. If later burials were made in the vault, the original bones were either pushed aside or moved, together with their gifts, towards the back of the chamber. In the case that the house was sold and the family moved, the remains of the dead could be taken with them to their new home.

More modest burials consisted of simple rectangular graves built from mud bricks set on edge beneath the floors of rooms, preferably in the living quarters of

Left In many of the burials the deceased was buried holding a bowl

the house. A shaft was dug a metre or two below the floor and lined with bricks to form a small chamber. Once the deceased had been placed there with his burial goods, the tomb was closed and sealed and the floor repaved.

The most humble version of interment was a simple earth grave, with the corpse wrapped in a shroud and reed mats to give at least some protection from the soil. Large potsherds could be placed above or beneath the body for further protection. When available, large, complete vessels could be laid together mouth to mouth to construct a makeshift coffin. Children in particular were buried in complete pots, in a flexed, almost fetal position.

Cremation of the dead was rarely practised by the Assyrians as it involved the destruction of the body, which was important in the afterlife. However, cremation burials were discovered in Ziyaret Tepe, both as primary burials and as burials in urns. The funerary vessel was often pierced by up to three holes – most likely to allow the spirit to move freely. Cremation appears to be a local burial custom, possibly under Aramean influence from the west, although this remains debatable: there was a long tradition of cremating the dead in Eastern Anatolia from the late 3rd millennium onwards, even before the advent of the Arameans.

Above A dish that once contained offerings for the deceased

Right A double-pot burial containing ashes from a cremation

Below A plan of the burial from under the floor in Operation M

1 Beaker vessel	11 Fibula
2 Cylinder-seal	12 Cylinder-seal
3 Bowl/vessel	13 Fibula
4 Stone pendant	14 Pendant
5 Iron pendants/ blade	15 Iron artefact
	16 Stones
6 Earrings	17 Artefact/slag
7 Iron artefact	18-26 Beads
8 Fibula pin	27 Stone find
9 Iron blade	
10 Ring	

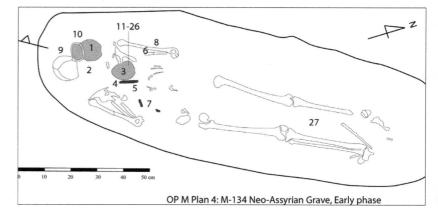

OP M Plan 4: M-134 Neo-Assyrian Grave, Early phase

Top left
Bronze fibula
with a clasp
in the form of
a hand

Left
An assortment
of beads

Below left
Our physical
anthropologist
Sandra Lösch
at work

Below right
Cylinder-seal
from the
Operation
Q Gate

0   1   2 cm

The gods of the land

Assyrians followed a polytheistic religion with a host of major and minor gods. At the top was Aššur, the city god of the original capital, Assur, and very much rooted in that city. Below Aššur came a tier of deities of whom the most prominent were Nabû, the god of writing (and therefore destinies), the moon god, Sin, the sun god, Šamaš, and the rain god, Adad. Nergal is an interesting case – he was a god of farmers but also, because men tilling the land also formed the army in the summer, a god of war and death. The most powerful female deity was Ishtar, a goddess pre-eminent in both love and war. Ishtar had many forms. There were, for example, separate avatars of Ishtar in Assur, Nineveh and Erbil, each of these having principal shrines in their home towns as well as enclave shrines in the other cities. It may well be that Ishtar was also the tutelary deity of Tušhan – at any rate, a priest of Ishtar of Nineveh is mentioned in the texts – but this is not certain, and it is worth mentioning that alongside all the things we discovered at Ziyaret Tepe, we did not locate the site of the ancient temple which the city must have had.

Apart from the Assyrian presence, Tušhan will also have been home to a range of other religious observations. Arameans, who we know were in the city as a result of both deportations and earlier incursions, also followed a polytheistic religion, albeit with a smaller pantheon than the Assyrians. While we have not found any indisputable evidence for Aramean cults at Tušhan, it may be that

Above
This tablet indicates the presence at Tušhan of a Shubrian augur, a specialist in predicting the future by observing the movements of birds

Left
This cylinder-seal depicts symbols of a number of the major gods of Assyria: the winged disk over the sacred tree is the symbol of the supreme god, Aššur; the crescent represents the moon god, Sin, and the star the goddess Ishtar; the deity denoted by the rhombus has, however, not yet been identified

Right
This figurine of
the dwarf god,
Bes, from a
burial in the
lower town,
indicates that
Egyptian elements
had permeated the
religious beliefs
of the land

Below
Burials found at Ziyaret Tepe in
which the body was cremated in a
grave pit with accompanying goods
– as in this painting by Dr Mary
Shepperson – may reflect the influence
of Aramean religious practices

the cremation burials betray an adoption of an Aramean practice (though, for all we know, the rites performed at the graveside may still have been Assyrian).

The indigenous Shubrians probably followed an offshoot of Hurrian religion, but with the goddess Pirengir at its head. Their seers had a particular expertise in augury (divining the future through monitoring the movement of birds), as mentioned in texts from both Ziyaret Tepe and Nimrud. An Egyptian element is hinted at by the figurine of the dwarf god Bes.

Lastly, deportees brought into Tušhan will have brought their own gods too. In the case of Babylonians, the chief deities were really the same as those of the Assyrian pantheon. The population group we believe to have been transported from the Zagros, on the other hand, will have had their own indigenous gods, although we have no information on who these deities were.

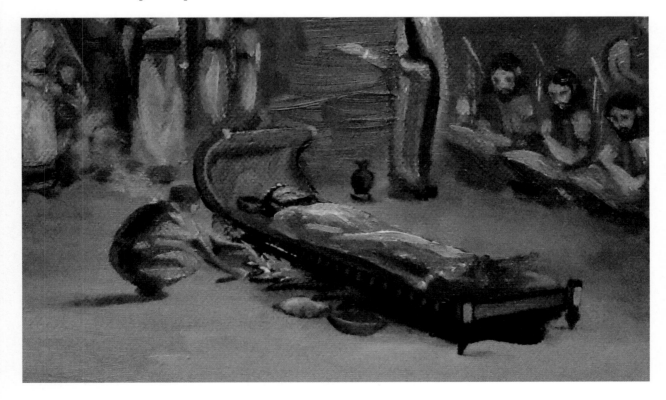

16.22
15.08
13.95
12.81
11.68
10.54
9.41
8.27
7.14
6.00
4.87
3.73
2.60
ohm

Above The bend
in the city wall
exposed at
Operation Y

The Tušhan city wall

Like all major cities of the time, Tušhan was protected by a fortification wall. Although the wall must originally have stood many metres high, the remains are now so eroded that they are visible only as a very low rise in the topography or not at all. The first definitive evidence for the walls came with the magnetic gradiometry surveys carried out at the southern edge of the lower town, which indicated the existence of a substantial wall running in an east-west direction. The results from the electrical-resistivity survey confirmed this interpretation, along with the presence of a gate. Subsequently our excavations impinged upon the wall in four areas: Operations D, K, Q and Y. The most extensive investigation was in Operation K, where a section through the wall revealed that it was just under 3m wide. It was built into a foundation trench dug into a terrace fill, and was protected by a

Right Resistivity map of the southwestern lower town, showing the wall running diagonally across the bottom of the image

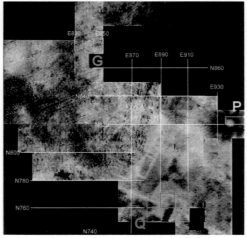

surrounding ditch, whose original width is difficult to establish but which must have been imposing. Whether or not this ditch was flooded to create a moat is something we were not able to determine. In any case, the digging of the ditch dovetailed very neatly with the construction of the wall, the earth from the former being used to make the bricks for the latter. The dimensions of the mud bricks are 38–40 x 38–40 x 12–13cm, with 4–9cm thick mud-mortar joins between the bricks. The whole circuit of the wall around Ziyaret Tepe comes to about 2km. While there is no preserved evidence for its height, it was probably in the order of 7–8m.

In addition to the Khabur Gate excavated in Operation Q, there must have been a gate on the northern side and perhaps on the other two sides as well. The wall was supported by watchtowers and by regularly spaced rectangular projecting buttresses. In some places there were rooms built up against the wall, no doubt for the use of the soldiers on duty. It will have been important, though, that these additions did not conflict with the clearway, a 3m-wide open zone that ran around the city on the inside of the wall, maintained to guarantee free movement in times of emergency. It is interesting to note that just such a clearway is also evident in the geophysical mapping of the lower town at the site of Zincirli – ancient Sam'al – in Gaziantep province.

Right The Assyrian army besieging a city; bas-relief from the palace of Ashurnasirpal II in Nimrud

Below Section across the fortification wall at Operation K, with the walls of the barracks blocks to the right

Below Right The Shamash Gate of Nineveh, as restored by Iraqi archaeologists

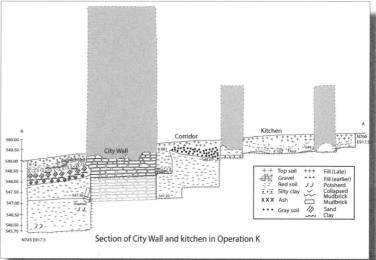

Section of City Wall and kitchen in Operation K

Forts along the River Tigris

Upon annexing a new territory an immediate task for the new Assyrian administration was to secure it. In general the first step was to construct a system of forts, preparing the way for the establishment of small agrarian communities. The programme entailed the construction of a walled city with a palace and royal stele, mansions for the elite and perhaps a temple. Newly transplanted settlers, whether Assyrians or deportees, were given grants of land in the surrounding territory, providing both the agricultural base for the settlement and seasonal manpower for the army.

In the case of Tušhan, it must have seemed Assyria had reached its natural limit, at least in this part of the Empire, and the cuneiform texts tell of a string of forts constructed along the Tigris frontier east of Amidu (Diyarbakır): Sinabu, Tidu and Tušhan itself. These correspond to the three archaeological sites of Pornak, Üçtepe and Ziyaret Tepe, all of which show signs of major Assyrian occupation. The importance of these forts is reflected in the letters of the royal correspondence from the governors of Tušhan, which usually employ the greeting formula: 'The forts and the land of the king, my lord, are well.'

Life on the northern frontier was not always quiet. An eye had to be kept on the neighbouring states, particularly Shubria in the north and Urartu to the northeast, monitoring their troop movements and bringing people and livestock south of the Tigris when trouble threatened. As one scholar has aptly put it, 'The "Great Game" of Assyrian times – complete with spies, assassinations and fugitives – was played out in the north.'

The southern gate to the city

We were originally attracted to the area of the southern gate by the results of the magnetometry and resistivity surveys. In both of these images the line of the city wall can clearly be seen, astride which is a large rectangular structure which could only be a gate.

But there are numerous issues to which remote sensing cannot supply the answers. Was the gate a single-chambered structure or did it have multiple chambers? Might there be evidence for phasing and rebuildings? Nor, of course, can remote sensing provide artefactual and ecofactual material. In these circumstances the decision was made to undertake a major excavation. The aim was to completely excavate this gateway through all phasings down to foundation level, in order to gain insights into its complete occupational and architectural history, and to recover a full record of the associated small finds, ceramic

Left A quiet day on the walls, as visualised by Dr Mary Shepperson

Right Early-morning light casts long shadows on the excavations of the city wall

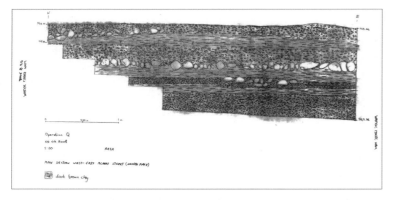

Above
Dr MacGinnis
examines the
section through
the road to the
city gate

Right Plan of
the layout of
the gate in its
third building
phase, showing
the slabs paving
the threshold
and the
occupational
features in the
eastern chamber

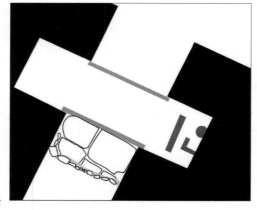

sequence and ecofactual material.

The excavations revealed that there were four main phases of construction, each marked by a considerable raising of the floor level. As Tušhan was refounded by Ashurnasirpal II in 882 BC and was occupied until 611 BC – a period of 271 years – the implication is that each phase was in use for a period of approximately 65–70 years. The fact that the cobble packing laid down for the Phase IV street contained a large number of broken 'Hands of Ishtar' suggests that these were decorative elements of the Phase III gate. A section cut through the outer street also evidenced four major phases, correlating with the sequence in the interior of the gate. In Phase III the approach to the outer threshold was reinforced with massive stone slabs sloping down to the threshold itself. Signs of wear on these slabs indicated wheeled traffic with an axial span of 2m. In at least the final phase the street ran out between two projecting walls flanking the gate.

Plentiful evidence was recovered for the domestic use of the gate chambers, particularly in the eastern chamber. The Phase III chamber had a bench and a hearth protected by an L-shaped installation. Two 'knuckle bones' (actually the unfused astragali of sheep) found on the floor were used in gaming – something attested from the time of Homer onwards. One can conjure up images of soldiers on night duty, huddled over the fire and whiling away the hours at dice.

On the inside of the city wall were the remains of a small complex built up against the gate. The rooms of this complex must surely have been for the use of the soldiers on duty at the gate, either rooms to which the soldiers might retire when their watch was complete or perhaps an office for their superiors. A small flask found in the mud-brick collapse is illustrative of the type of small possession that they might have kept about their person.

Above
Final photograph of the Operation Q gate, showing evidence from multiple phases

Right
A typical day in the life of the gate, as recreated by Dr Mary Shepperson

Below Princes playing at knuckle bones - a sculpture from Neo-Hittite Carchemish

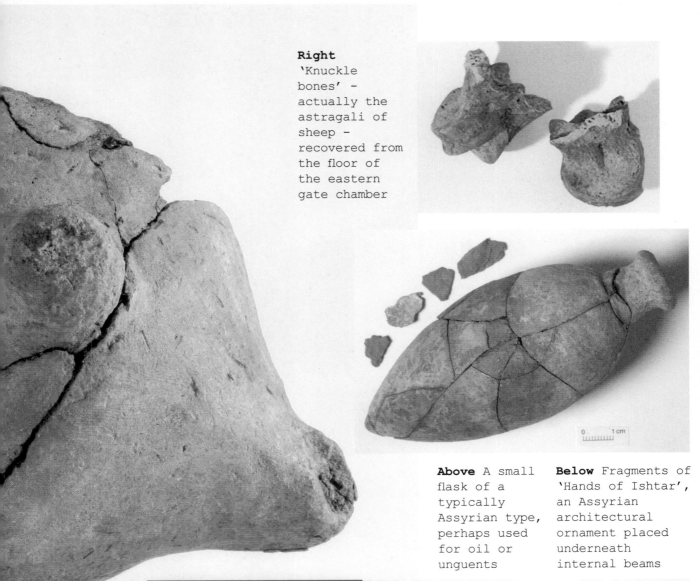

Right
'Knuckle bones' - actually the astragali of sheep - recovered from the floor of the eastern gate chamber

Above A small flask of a typically Assyrian type, perhaps used for oil or unguents

Below Fragments of 'Hands of Ishtar', an Assyrian architectural ornament placed underneath internal beams

Above
A 'pig pot', an amusing drinking vessel of a form with a long pedigree behind it

The military barracks by the city wall

The excavations along the city wall uncovered a structure tentatively identified as a military barracks. The complex consisted of eight rooms built around a semi-open space. It is evident from the tannurs (ovens) that two rooms (A and F) were used for cooking purposes. A series of five rooms measuring approximately 4 x 3m are laid out in a row parallel to the city wall. The floors were covered with a layer of ash and mud-brick collapse up to 25cm thick. One of the rooms, Room C, had three graves dug into the floor. Finds in Room A included conical stone and clay tokens and beads, and sherds of Neo-Assyrian pottery, including

Right
The director observes progress in Operation K

Below
The plan of the barracks as uncovered over three seasons of excavation

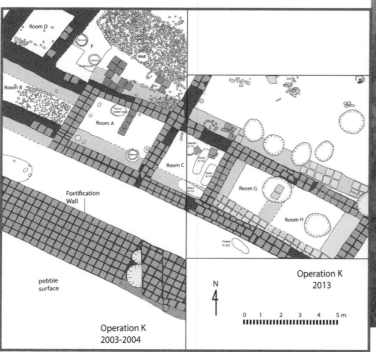

palace-ware goblets. Other finds include a fragment of a fibula, a needle, part of a stone vessel and a clay bulla bearing the impression of a stamp-seal. Most of the rooms contained sherds of bowls with thickened rims, very likely coarse tableware. To the north is a courtyard measuring 4.40 x 5.80m, paved with pebbles and reused bricks and with a well in the middle. It is the only area in which remains of large jars were found, suggesting that this space may have functioned in a storage capacity.

Below all this was a lower phase with remarkable similarity to the upper phase. Indeed, it is clear that the lower phase was levelled down to its foundations and a new

Above
Elegant profiles: sherds of typical Neo-Assyrian bowls

building, shifted some 80–90cm to the south, constructed on top with the same plan. Room functions were not changed – for example, rooms with tannurs (Rooms A and F) in the earlier level had tannurs again in the later level. Room C contained burials underneath its floors in both levels.

This sequence mirrors what happened elsewhere on the site, where numerous other structures, including the city walls, were similarly levelled to their foundations and rebuilt after a short period. These rebuildings evidently followed a crisis and subsequent destruction that occurred at the beginning of the 8th century BC. The proximity of the structure to the city's south gate, as

well as its being built parallel to the city wall – and most importantly the fact that a series of rooms have a direct outdoor exit – do not give the impression of a normal household plan. We think for these reasons that these may be the remains of a military barracks.

Beer for the troops

Beer has been softening the edges of daily life since the emergence of civilisation. The very first written records, proto-cuneiform texts from Uruk (in southern Iraq) from the late 4th millennium BC, already document the production of beer.

In ancient Mesopotamia beer could be made from barley or emmer, but also from dates. It was a thick and cloudy brew with mostly a low alcoholic content. It could be flavoured with the addition of honey, date or grape syrup, or herbs and spices, but it had such heavy sediment that it had to be strained or drunk through a straw. But beer was cheap and easy to make and as a result was often issued in rations. While consuming wine was more the preserve of the elite, the soldiers stationed in Tušhan would have been more familiar with beer.

Elite residences

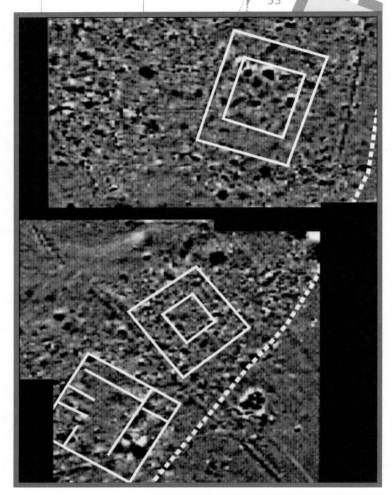

In the course of work at Ziyaret Tepe we came down onto the remains of elite residences in several locations. The first to be investigated was in Operation G, an area we were originally drawn to by the results of the magnetometry survey, which suggested the presence of coherent architectural remains. In the end we were able to expose the entire plan of the Operation G residence – and it was encouraging to note that the features interpreted as walls in the magnetometry survey corresponded closely to the plan actually recovered!

The building demonstrated a number of characteristics typical of high-status architecture. First of all, just its size: 25 x 38m. Second, the impressive quality of the masonry, with walls up to 1.8m thick built of large (41 x 41 x 12–14cm) bricks made out of tough red clay which had been freshly dug, rather than recycled old mud-brick material. Thirdly, the presence of pithoi (huge jars), indicating the storage of agricultural surplus. And, fourthly, the presence of a pebble mosaic pavement. The residence had 11 rooms. The main entrance was on the east through a doorway paved with stone slabs. This led through a hall into a central courtyard, around which the remaining rooms were arranged.

Two soundings were carried out in Operation G. The first of these was undertaken in order to determine the depth of the building's foundations, which turned out to be five courses of bricks deep, about 70cm. The second sounding was carried out in order to establish the overall depth of cultural deposits in the site, which proved to be a little over 3m.

128

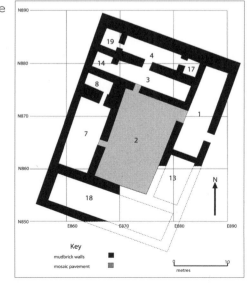

Right Plan of the the elite residence at Operation G/R indicating the mud-brick walls and the position of the mosaic floor

Left The magnetometry map, highlighting features thought to be high-status residences in the southeastern lower town

39

E830

Key

walls ▪

pavement ▪

0

metres

Right
Final photograph in Operation G/R, showing the impressive pebble mosaic cut by a later pit

Operation M

The first investigations in Operation M, in the central lower town, south of the main mound, took place in 2004 in order to ground–truth a linear feature visible in the geophysical prospections. That excavation discovered a deposit of cobbles and pebbles up to 70cm thick, clearly the remains of a street – and so confirming the geophysical results – but it also produced evidence for mud-brick architecture alongside.

In 2012 we returned to the area in order to investigate further. There proved to be the remains of a high-status residence with walls a metre thick. Parts of two rooms were excavated. While the data was not sufficient to identify the function of these rooms, the most significant finds were two graves cut into the floor. The first contained two child burials, with a few accompanying grave goods. The second grave, of an adult man, was much more lavish, the goods including cylinder-seals, iron blades, an iron needle, bronze earrings, a bronze fibula, a frit pendant of the Egyptian dwarf god, Bes, two ceramic vessels and a large number of beads. The finds from these graves date the building to the Neo-Assyrian period; the fibula in particular dates to the 8th century BC.

Operation U

The third area where we investigated a high-status residence was Operation U, in the far southeast corner of the lower town. We were keen to work in this area as it was a part of the site where we had not hitherto conducted any excavations, but our interest was particularly focused by the results of the mapping by magnetometry carried out in 2009, which had produced indications that there might be a series of substantial residences situated here, close up to the city wall. However, intriguing as these images were, they were faint and in need of corroboration. Accordingly, a main aim of the work in Operation U was to further investigate these features. We approached this by a combined plan of firstly resurveying the area using resistivity and then following this up with targeted excavation in order to ground-truth the results. The plan of the building found in excavation – after first encountering two Late Roman levels – corresponded exactly to the geophysical imaging. To the west of the building was a street with a metalling of pebbles thickly set in heavy brown clay which contained some excellent archaeozoological evidence in terms of bones, some quite large, lying pressed into the surface.

Wine... the drink of the elite

The history of wine goes back a long way. Traces of wine have been found in jars from Neolithic levels in Georgia and Iran, from where it spread throughout the Near East. It was popular in Assyria. The excavations of the French archaeologist Botta in the 19th century uncovered the remains of the royal wine cellar of Sargon II at his capital, Khorsabad, while British excavations at Nimrud recovered lists detailing the issue of wine to functionaries and dignitaries attending the Assyrian court. A famous relief from Nineveh shows Ashurbanipal reclining in his garden, bowl in hand. Perhaps he was drinking wine from Izalla, known to have been particularly prized.

Left
Cuneiform text from Nimrud recording the issue of wine to courtiers

Right
Bronze bowl and strainer, from a hoard associated with one of the cremation burials

Above
Ashurbanipal relaxing with his queen and a bowl of wine
Right Our own garden scene - the patio in the dig-house

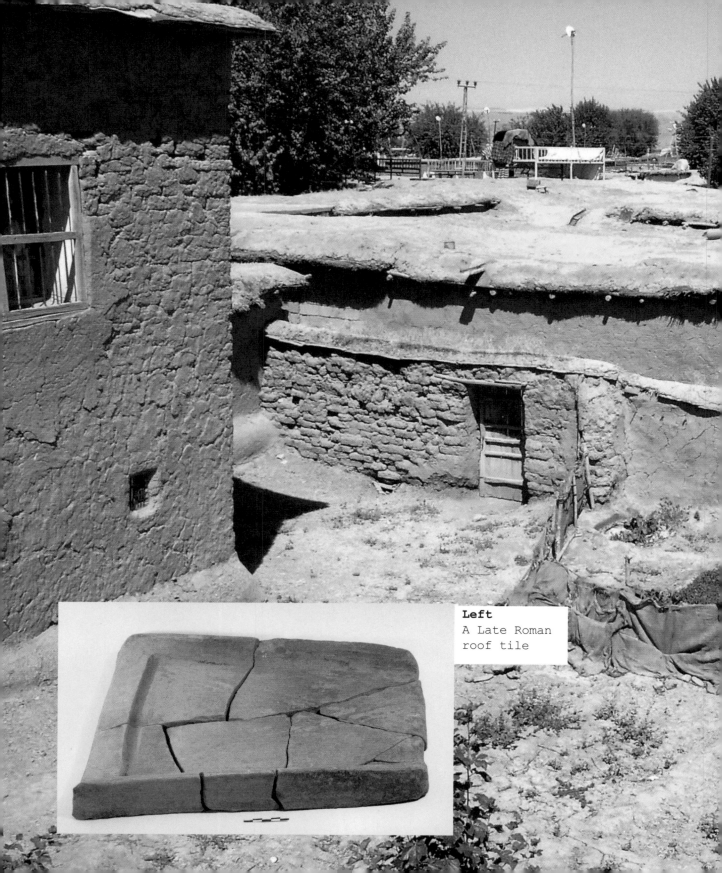

Left
A Late Roman
roof tile

A traditional mud-brick house in the village, with its roof made of mud plastered on a layer of reeds resting on wooden poles

Evolution of the roof

The traditional mud roof is a technology that has lasted thousands of years. It is made by stretching beams across a room, overlaying them with mats and covering these with mud. The mud would need to be replastered from time to time, and after heavy rain would be evened out with a roof roller. At Ziyaret Tepe we found evidence of a second technology: roof tiles. These date to the Late Roman period, and are a distinctive feature of that occupation. In the modern village, examples of traditional mud roofs do remain, but technology has moved on again and the majority are made using today's favoured material, cement.

Right A roof roller found in a pit cutting into the Late Roman levels

A tiled roof in the modern village of Tepe

134

Work in progress on the administrative complex in Operation G/R. Note the bathroom tiled with baked bricks

The administrative complex

T he excavation of the administrative complex in Operation G (later renamed Operation R) was one of the major accomplishments of the project. Two factors led to choosing this part of the site for the focus of work. Firstly, this area showed up in the contour survey as a distinct sub-mound in its own right. Secondly, the results of the magnetometry survey imaged what appeared to be the remains of coherent architecture. In the end we worked at Operation G/R over a period of more than 10 years, exposing an area of over 2,000sq m. In the course of this we uncovered almost the complete plan of the building – though we never actually saw it like that, as we had to backfill all the excavation squares at the end of each season.

The complex is laid out around two courtyards, both paved with black and white pebble mosaics. In the order of 20 rooms are arranged around these courtyards. The main entrance is to the west, consisting of a baked-brick porch outside a stone-paved threshold 1.7m wide. The long room

136

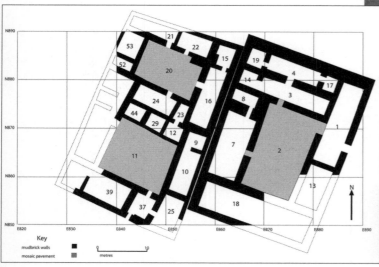

Key
mudbrick walls
mosaic pavement

metres

Left
The combined plan of the Operation G/R architecture, with the administrative complex on the left and an elite residence on the right

across the courtyard from this (Room 16) was clearly a reception room, with a bathroom (Room 15) attached. This room, incidentally, provided clear evidence for a major remodelling of the building: the original baked-brick floor was covered over by a thick layer of grey plaster with a white-painted surface, onto which was painted a design of concentric rectangles in black.

In other locations it was clear that the original walls had been razed almost to floor level and new walls rebuilt almost exactly on top, although a few degrees off. While we cannot ascribe an exact function to all of the rooms, the majority we believe to be storerooms and offices. Of exceptional importance is the unit made up by Rooms 9 and 10, where the cuneiform tablets were found: the arrangement – a long chamber with a smaller chamber at the end – is a typical layout for archival suites. The contents of these tablets, together with the presence of sealings, weights and a mass of accounting tokens, demonstrate the administrative function of the complex.

The building was also home to numerous pithoi – some let into the floor and some lying on the floor, evidently waiting to be installed – which would have been used for the storage of grain and perhaps oil; one of these was particularly unusual, being moulded in one piece with its base. As to the precise identification of the building, one suggestion is that it was connected with the temple of Ishtar; perhaps this is supported by the presence of numerous loom weights, indicating that weaving, an activity characteristically carried out by temple dependants, took place in the location. Another suggestion is that it was the office of the city treasurer.

Right
Detail of stamped
pithos sherd

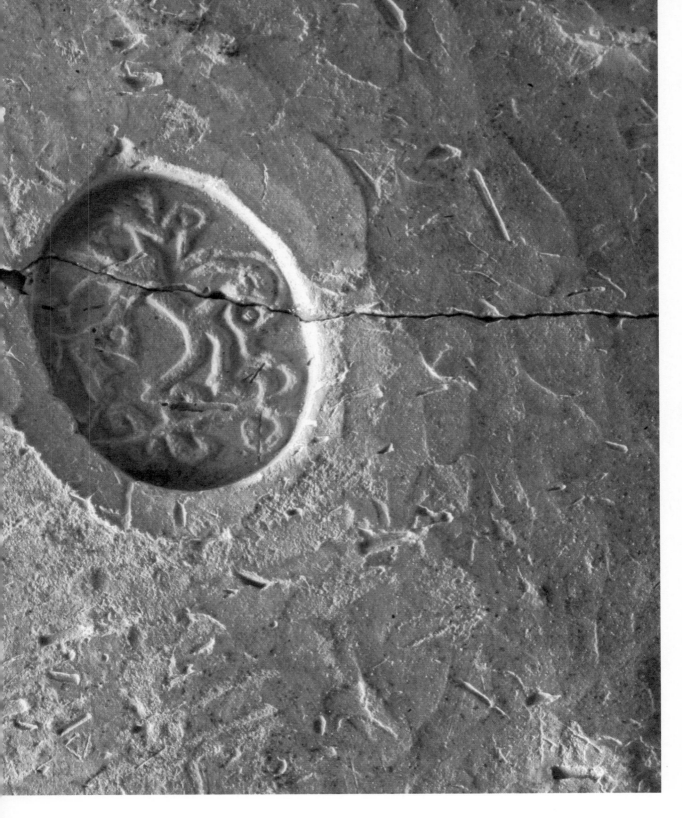

Above Excavations in Operation G/R. A pebble mosaic can be seen on the left; another mosaic is emerging below the pithos

Right Close-up of the handled pithos. The surface on which it rested, the fourth mosaic pavement to be discovered, was not excavated in its entirety

Left The drainage system under the pavement in Bathroom 15

Above The baked-brick pavement of Bathroom 15. Note the drain with stopper still in place on the right

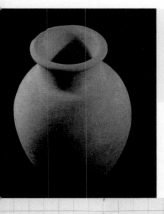

Above Cylinder-seal depicting a worshipper before a stylised sacred tree and a winged horse

Above
A typical Assyrian smaller storage vessel

Right
A pithos from Operation G

Above left
A bronze 'omphalos' bowl from an Achaemenid grave cut into the mud-brick collapse of the complex

Far left
Tablet ZTT 1, recording the receipt of grain, probably from outlying farmsteads; it is thought to date to 611 BC, the very year in which Tušhan fell to the Babylonians

Left Triangular dockets such as these were typically employed for recording loans of grain. This one has an added interest as it is the only text found at Ziyaret Tepe which mentions the governor

Right
Fragment of an ivory comb

Ziyaret Tepe 2002
Op. G Tr. N860E850
Loc. G-710
ZT 12002
Storage vessel

The pebble mosaics

Among the numerous defining features of Assyrian elite architecture, there is one that stands out unmistakably: the pebble mosaic pavements. These are found across the Empire, or at least the northern half of the Empire, from southeastern Turkey through northern Syria to northern Iraq, used in palaces, temples, major administrative buildings and mansions of the elite.

The first chequerboard mosaic pavements to be discovered were those in the Assyrian capital city of Assur, on the Tigris, and at the major provincial sites of Arslan Tash and Til Barsip in Syria, all in the earlier part of the 20th century. In the 1980s a splendid example was uncovered by the British expedition at the site of Tille, on the Euphrates in Adıyaman province, in the salvage operations conducted in advance of the Birecik Dam. Most recently of all, in 2014 the ▷ 149

Above The pavement in Courtyard 2, discovered in the very first weeks of working in Operation G

Above right The pavement in Courtyard 20

Previous pages and inset above Detail of the mosaic pavement from Courtyard 11

Above
A section of the mosaic pavement in Courtyard 20; the rectangle of larger stones in the foreground may be a marker for a grave

Right
A courtyard in the complex, as reconstructed by Dr Mary Shepperson

Above right
The wider context: pebbled mosaic pavements were a characteristic feature of the Assyrian presence across the Empire. This one was discovered at the site of Tille, in Adiyaman Province

excavations by Bologna University at Carchemish have revealed a fine chequerboard pavement, which formed part of the palace built there by Sargon II.

Into this pattern fit the pavements from Ziyaret Tepe. We were fortunate enough to discover numerous pavements of this type, three excavated in full and a fourth of which only a part was exposed. The first was uncovered in 2001, in the first season at Operation G, and its discovery was a welcome confirmation that the lower town was indeed the site of important Assyrian remains. In terms of design, the pavements can be made up of either just plain black and white squares, or of more elaborate designs, particularly St Andrew's (diagonal) crosses, with the squares made out of alternating triangles of black and white, and rosettes.

Finally, returning to the distribution of these pavements, they may possibly also have existed in the southern half of the Empire – down the Mediterranean coast in the west and in Babylonia in the east – although they have not yet been found. But extending these horizons in both directions, it is noteworthy that examples have been excavated both in Spain, at the site of Cástulo – the concept perhaps having been transmitted by the Phoenecians – and in western Iran at the site of Rabat Tepe.

Preparing food and drink

Food preparation and consumption in the Near East has remained very similar over time. Modifications to animal bones are generally considered good indicators of deliberate food-preparation activities. The slaughter, skinning and portioning of animals, and the cooking of the meat are all activities that are evident in the animal bones excavated from Ziyaret Tepe.

Modifications on bones are generally the result of butchering activities carried out as part of food-processing activities. Cut marks (slices on the bones from stone and metal knives and axes) are analysed by zooarchaeologists to determine the full process of food preparation. The burning of bones is generally the result of cooking activities reserved for the consumption of meat. Evidence of the burning of specimens is indicative of the bones being placed in hearths or fire pits for roasting. Bones with polish are sometimes identified as having been boiled in pots as part of stews.

Specific species consumed at Ziyaret Tepe include domestic animals such as cattle, sheep, goats, pigs and, to a much lesser extent, horses, donkeys and dogs. Wild species, eaten far less often, included large and small deer, boar, birds of several varieties, hares, foxes and turtles.

Animals are both food and symbol, and often social status can be equated with economic status, since specific species and meat portions are frequently regarded as high or low status. Animals such as wild deer and exotic birds were typically consumed by the elite, although this behaviour was also emulated by the lower orders. What is clear is that there was a well-defined division in society when it came to food at Ziyaret Tepe. Evidence was found that high-status species were consumed within the Bronze Palace and other elite residences at Tušhan.

Another indicator of status or wealth in ancient complex societies is the types of meat that were consumed. The analysis of body portions of animals allows for patterns to emerge regarding species taboos, preferences and wealth display, which can often be markers for status. At Ziyaret Tepe different portions of animals were uncovered and grouped into highly desired, heavily meat-bearing cuts; less desired, less meaty cuts; and the least desired cuts with only little meat. The most desirable portions were generally found in the elite parts of the settlement, while the poorer cuts of meat were found in the lower-stratum quarters.

Feasts

A variety of texts expound the luxurious and indulgent banquets laid out by the Assyrian kings. These festivities were a chance to display wealth through conspicuous consumption, and a concerted effort was made in delineating the gap between the elite and non-elite. Exotic animals such as monkeys and peacocks were displayed and consumed in staggeringly high numbers. Fresh herbs and exotic spices from foreign lands were used in magnificent culinary meals and vast amounts of wine were consumed on a daily basis. It is thought that only the top rung of the royal family, courtiers, governors and other important officials were allowed to attend these banquets.

For the lower-stratum families or individuals, however, the diet was relatively bland. It consisted of very little

Above
Necmi, our
inestimable cook
- the title hardly
does him justice
- a true genius who
kept us fed and
happy through one
season after
another

Left
Necmi preparing
yet another
feast, here with
the help of his
daughter Tuğba

meat, with a high percentage of cereals, fish and vegetables, with little spicing. These consumption patterns are also evident at Ziyaret Tepe.

Turning to religious provisions, according to texts, offerings for the gods included sheep, goats, cattle, birds, breads, vegetables and wine, all of which have been found in the Bronze Palace at Ziyaret Tepe.

Above Dinner is served to the team in the dig-house

Left Local traditions in food preparation continue unchanged

Bread

Of all the ways in which societies manifest their distinctiveness, one of the most striking is bread – it is one of the great cultural indicators. For archaeologists this poses a problem, as it is rare that remains of bread are actually preserved in the material record. To some extent this is compensated for by information in cuneiform texts, which contain words for many different types of bread. Every ethnic group has its own sorts of bread, and this is just as true today as it was in antiquity.

Left
Circular grinding
stones used in
the village for
milling grain

Above a traditional
wood-fired oven
used to bake bread.
Note the loaves on
the inside

Left The remains of
an ancient hearth in
Operation Q

Chapter 4
Ziyaret Tepe reveals its rich and varied finds

The Tušhan archive

In the study of ancient Assyria we are fortunate that the archaeological remains are illuminated by the rich record of the texts. At Ziyaret Tepe we were lucky enough to find a large number of cuneiform tablets. The majority of these are from the archive discovered in Rooms 9 and 10 of the administrative complex in the lower town. Altogether 28 tablets were recovered. Originally stored either in baskets or on shelves, they were found on the floors of the rooms in a fragmentary and parlous state requiring very careful handling, first allowed to dry out slowly, then baked under controlled conditions.

The contents of the tablets include references to movements of grain, the loan of a slave, lists of personnel, the resettlement of people and a census listing officers and their agricultural holdings. But the majority deal with transactions of barley – deliveries from outlying farmsteads, loans and payments for rations – and there can be no doubt that this was a major concern of the establishment. This conclusion is also indicated by the presence of the numerous pithoi (huge storage jars) in the complex. The amounts of grain listed in the texts vary from just

Left ZTT 22: a letter written as the Assyrian Empire reached its end, reporting that the military infrastructure of Tušhan had collapsed

Below Prof. Simo Parpola, one of the world's leading experts on ancient Assyrian, deciphers the archive

2 to a staggering 38,000 litres. But the office handled multiple jurisdictions and, in addition to the administration of grain, had responsibilities concerning the harem, the temple of Ishtar and the military. Overall, the evidence of the texts gives an excellent overview of the commodities handled in the building: grain, metals, woods, wool, textiles and leather. A degree of corroboration comes from the discovery of a stone 'duck weight' found there, which weighed 30kg, corresponding to one

Right Dr John MacGinnis studies a tablet from the later excavations

Assyrian talent. This would have been used for the weighing of metal, textiles and bitumen. Another artefact of interest is the unusual tablet ZTT 31, which had been deliberately pierced, evidently to allow a cord to be passed through so it could be attached as a tag to a container or bundle of materials.

The fall of the Empire

An extraordinary feature of these texts is that they date to the very end of the Empire, i.e. just before and just after the fall of Nineveh in 612 BC. The occurrence of the official Nabû-tapputi-alik in ZTT 4 dates that text to 613 BC, while the occurrence of Ashur-šarrani, whom the distinguished Finnish Assyriologist Simo

Parpola dates to 611 BC, is unique.

The fact that the great majority of the texts are of a routine nature suggests the Assyrians were at this stage still expecting to regain control of their Empire. But other texts clearly relate to the struggle at hand. One example is ZTT 8, which records an issue of armour to three individuals who are evidently not necessarily expected to return. The issue of a large sum of copper to a prophet recorded in ZTT 25 is interpreted by Parpola as a reward for a prophesy on the eve of a major engagement. Even more dramatic is ZTT 22, a letter written by a certain Mannu-ki-libbali to a senior official, perhaps the city treasurer. Evidently Mannu-ki-libbali had been asked to muster a unit of chariotry. However, the entire structure to support such an order had collapsed.

Above Tom Burns excavating tablets in Room 10, the larger of the two archive chambers

Preceding page The archives from the administrative complex in the lower town, a collection of tablets offering a unique insight into the final years of the Assyrian Empire

Above These ivory pieces may have been hinges from a set of writing boards

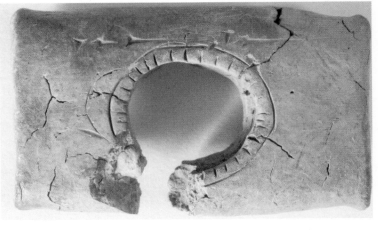

Right ZTT 31: a tag deliberately pierced to allow a cord to be run through it

Seals and sealings

The act of sealing, whether it be documents or the door of a museum storeroom, is still a highly official and important action constituting an expression of personal authority. In general, seals – the Assyrian word was *kunukku* – were owned by one person, and were even buried with them. Finding seals passed down as heirlooms within families is consequently the exception rather than the rule. As with losing a credit card today, the loss of an official seal could cause great trouble and was proclaimed publicly to avoid fraudulent use.

Seals could be worn on a string around the neck or pinned to a garment. In the Assyrian period the use of cylinder-shaped seals was most common. These could easily be rolled over the still-malleable surface of clay tablets so that the image would repeat itself. For the modern archaeologist, the overlapping of different seals is a great challenge, for it obscures the details of the image, often making it very difficult to identify the separate seals.

With the spread of Aramaic – which was written in ink on parchment or leather rather than on clay – the use of stamp-seals became more popular. Seal-rings, rare in Assyrian times, became much more popular later on, in the Hellenistic period and after.

Sealing a clay tablet was comparable to signing a document. In the event that an individual did not have their own seal, they could make an impression with the hem of their garment or with their fingernail instead, and impressions of this type are often found. In the Assyrian period, only the seals of higher-ranking officials were engraved with the name of the owner. In the absence of this, the seal had to be identified by the imagery alone or by an epigraph – a label written on the tablet next to the impression of the seal, stating to whom it belonged. In contracts the witnesses would be named in the main body of the text and their individual seal impressions then specifically identified. Seal impressions are also found on vessels, where their function was to identify the individual or institutional owner.

The most elaborate Assyrian seals are works of art in their own right. The use of hard (and often colourful) stones allowed for the engraving of finely detailed imagery, such as the worshipper in front of a seated female deity seen in the image to the right, which was delicately modelled with a drill. The most common motifs in Assyrian seals are worshippers flanking a tree, and banquet scenes. A cheaper alternative to stone was frit, an artificial material formed of sintered quartz, which could be coloured and glazed. The large group of Assyrian frit cylinder-seals found across the Empire almost invariably show the motif of a hunter shooting an animal – snake, bull or gazelle – which apparently alludes to some episode in mythology no longer decipherable to us today. Another typical motif depicts waterbirds or ostriches, producing an endless row of birds once the seal is rolled out. These frit cylinder-seals appear to have been made in the same workshops as a group of knobbed conical stamp-seals, which depict a single star, scorpion or bird, as if an abbreviation of the repeating motifs of the cylinder-seals.

Clockwise from top: cylinder-seal from a grave in Operation Q showing worshippers each side of a stylised tree, with a winged disc hovering above; modern wax and lead sealings; a stamp-seal (which may also have served as an amulet) from Operation R; a limestone cylinder-seal depicting an archer (not shown) shooting a winged snake; clay sealing from Operation R – note the impressions of cuneiform writing from an inscription cut into the seal itself; a modern reconstruction of the way in which sealed clay was used for securing doors in antiquity; a stamp-seal from a cremation burial showing a worshipper before a seated deity

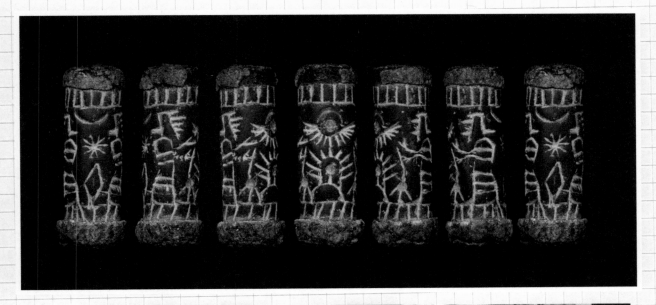

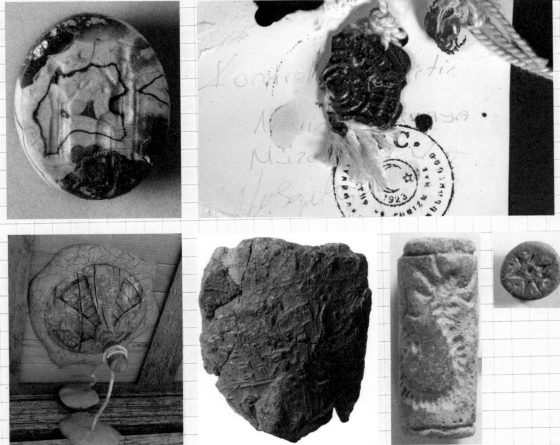

Weights and measures

The ancient inhabitants of Tušhan conducted business amongst themselves and with neighbouring cities and traders. They had a collection of equipment and procedures for making transactions efficient, standardised and, hopefully, fair. The evidence for this best attested in the material record comes in the form of weights.

Two excellent examples of standardised weights were found at Ziyaret Tepe in the course of the excavations. The larger of the two, from the lower town, weighed 30kg, equivalent to one Assyrian 'light' talent. The smaller one, found in the palace, came in at 1.1kg, equivalent to one Assyrian 'heavy' mina. Both these units of measurement were standard across the Empire: one talent was equal to 30 minas. Cuneiform documents attest to the use of weights in activities occurring in the Operation G/R administrative complex, and multiple texts make use of the mina unit in the quantification of commodities measured by weight.

Our time spent in the markets of local villages and towns also involved the use of the standardized weights and measures still in use today. Even on site, we made good use of metal two-pan scales and a sets of standard metal weights to weigh pottery. Electronic scales could fail in the heat or their batteries could run out. The metal scales were always available and functioning.

Left
A scene from the Rassam Obelisk showing booty being weighed before an Assyrian official

Measuring systems

The metric systems of ancient Mesopotamia present a famously complex picture. Over the 3,000 years when cuneiform writing was in use, a bewildering variety of systems were utilised for recording different metrics in different places. Fortunately, by the Neo-Assyrian period the measurements for grain and commodities were comparatively straightforward. The basic unit was the *qû*, approximately one litre. Ten *qû* formed a *sūtu*, and ten *sūtu* formed a homer (*imēru*). This last word actually means 'donkey', the implication being that this was a standard donkey-load.

The development of systems of weight in ancient Mesopotamia also presents a varied picture (though perhaps a little less confusing than that of other areas such as surface mensuration). The basic unit was the *šiqlu* – the same word as shekel – equivalent to about 8.33g. The progression was then according to base 60:60 shekels made a mina (*mana*) and 60 minas made a talent (*biltu*). The mina and talent were therefore in the range of 0.5kg and 30kg respectively each. For more precise measurement the shekel was divided into 180 'grains' (*š'ēu*), a grain therefore equivalent to about 0.0463g.

● ● ● ● ● ● ● ●

Above
Traditional scales with weights, used by local shopkeepers for weighing vegetables - and by us for weighing our pottery

Right
A duck weight from Operation R - it weighed 30kg, exactly corresponding to an Assyrian talent

Tokens

From the cuneiform texts found at the site we know that there was a significant amount of storage and disbursement of commodities centred around the large structures in Operation G/R. While the results of these transactions were recorded on cuneiform tablets, the counting and weighing of the grain and other stored commodities would have required tools similar to those we still use today: weights and measures and temporary counting devices. In this respect, the corpus of clay tokens from Ziyaret Tepe is of extraordinary interest.

These simple, undecorated tokens come in a variety of basic geometric shapes: spheres, cones, cylinders, tetrahedra (pyramids) and others. What makes us sure that they were used in accounting, and that they were not just game pieces, is not only the sheer number – in the end nearly 500 were found – but the fact that the overwhelming majority were found in a building whose bureaucratic function is demonstrated by a range of artefacts of administrative culture including tablets, dockets, sealings and weights.

In fact, almost two-thirds of the tokens found at the site came from a single room in the administrative complex, Room 37. This is clearly not a coincidence. Room 37 controls the passage from a working entrance into the building to the archival chambers, strongly suggesting that the tokens were being employed to record information coming from outside the building – whether sacks of grain immediately outside, or reports on flocks out in the countryside – before this information was forwarded for entering in the cuneiform record-keeping. In other words, tokens constituted a system for keeping tallies and dynamic totals of

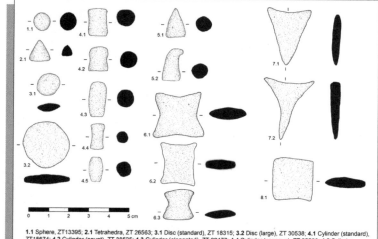

1.1 Sphere, ZT13395; 2.1 Tetrahedra, ZT 26563; 3.1 Disc (standard), ZT 18315; 3.2 Disc (large), ZT 30538; 4.1 Cylinder (standard), ZT15674; 4.2 Cylinder (squat), ZT 38525; 4.3 Cylinder (elongated), ZT 22477; 4.4 Cylinder (concave), ZT 25506; 4.5 Cylinder (convex), ZT 13362; 5.1 Cone, ZT15141; 5.2 Bent cone, ZT 13366; 6.1 Oxhide (square), ZT 12125; 6.2 Oxhide (rectangular, Tell Tayinat; 6.3 Oxhide (rectangular, flattened ends), ZT 30263; 7.1 Contracting triangle (concave triangle), Tell Tayinat; 7.2 "Bull's head" triangle (rounded triangle), Tell Tayinat; 8.1 Square (ZT 11187).

agricultural produce and livestock.

The system was flexible, could preserve information over extended periods of time and did not require literacy. While the precise meanings which the tokens encoded is not yet known – did different shapes represent different animals or commodities, or different quantities, or even an embodiment of both? – it should be stressed that the use of tokens has a long history in Mesopotamia, going back to the 4th millennium BC, when they are thought to have played a role in the process leading up to the invention of writing. Thereafter, the evidence for tokens continues sporadically into the 2nd millennium BC, when they are found still in use for recording movements of sheep and goats at the site of Nuzi in northeastern Iraq. But the fact that tokens were still used in the 1st millennium BC, and specifically in Neo-Assyrian administration, was unknown. The evidence from Ziyaret Tepe has been pivotal in demonstrating that this was the case.

Board games

From time to time in the excavations we would find baked bricks with a grid-like pattern scratched onto the surface. When cleaned and photographed, these inscribed marks outlined the playing surface of the 'Game of Ur', famously known from the beautiful inlaid board dating to the mid-3rd millennium BC found in the royal tombs excavated by Sir Leonard Woolley in the 1920s. While the example from Ur is made from such luxury materials as lapis lazuli and ivory, the scratched surface of our brick examples sufficed.

There are good parallels from other sites in Mesopotamia of the baked bricks used in paving courtyards having games scratched onto their surface – perhaps by the soldiers on duty or by visitors waiting for an appointment. At the site of Mari on the middle Euphrates, for example, one of the courtyards has five bricks with incised game-boards. These were all situated right against the walls, a place which would have been in the shade of canopies while at the same time not blocking movement through the courtyard. At the imperial capital of Khorsabad, even one of the colossal *lamassu* (winged bulls) which guarded the gates of the palace had the game scratched into its base.

The Game of Ur is what is traditionally known as a race game. The object is for two players to move their pieces, in this case multiple pieces per player, from one end of the board to the other. Movement is determined by some sort of random generator, that is to say dice or the like. The set from Ur came with pyramid-shaped dice, but 'knuckle bones' (actually the astragali, or ankle bones, of sheep) also made good dice. As regards the rules of the game, while there must have been variations across time and place, one set of rules has recently been deciphered from a tablet discovered in the British Museum.

In modern Tepe, of course, backgammon was the game par excellence, a defining pursuit of the villages' *çayhanes*. In the evening our team, too, liked to relax: here again backgammon was popular, and the game of Okey also became a favourite, with epic sessions played out after supper.

Above
The team play backgammon and a game called Okey at the end of a hard day's work

Following page
A deluxe game-board from the royal tombs at the city of Ur, from the mid-3rd millennium BC

165

Left
Game-boards scratched into bricks

Opposite
Administrative clay tokens

Artefacts of ivory and bone

Decorative inlays with pegs for fitting. The circles in the middle will have been filled with material of a contrasting colour

From prehistoric times onwards bone has been used in the making of artefacts. The distinctive feature of such artefacts is that the bone has been modified, whether by reshaping or by altering the surface by polishing or smoothing. While less common in the Iron Age than in earlier periods, numerous bone artefacts were uncovered by the excavations.

Bone was used for ornaments such as pendants, brooches, pins and bracelets. It was refashioned into tools, including spatulas and needles, and other items which suggest the practice of a further craft – awls for leatherwork and spindles for spinning wool. Additionally, bone (particularly antler) was also used as a platform for making other tools, and as a rubber for smoothing surfaces such as unfired ceramic pots and leather.

On a larger scale, antlers from red deer (*Cervus elaphus*) were used for digging implements and will often present with polished tines. The keratin sheaths from cattle horns were used for a variety of objects such as drinking cups, ornaments and decorations on clothing. Game pieces made from the astragali of sheep were uncovered in a relatively high frequency at Ziyaret Tepe, often highly polished or with perforations, possibly for use as dice. There are also interesting one-off artefacts, such as a polished lion bone and a sewing kit consisting of metal needles in a goose-bone case.

Above
An incised strip, probably for inlay

Right
Ivory spindle

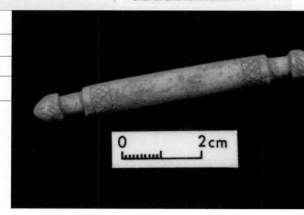

This page, clockwise from top right
The many uses of ivory: the shaft of a pin; make-up stick; blade; incised panels; loom weight

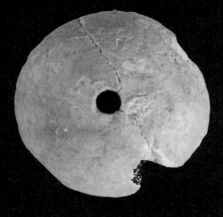

Textiles
and wool

Some of the first textiles produced in the Near East were made of linen, the fibre of the flax plant, found in Egypt from at least 7,000 years ago. It was not until around 2,000 years later that sheep's wool began to be used for making textiles and clothing.

Following their domestication in southwest Asia approximately 10,000 years ago, sheep were at first managed for their primary products (meat and hides), and it was not until the 'secondary products revolution', which took place around 5,000 years ago, that they were exploited for milk, traction and wool. Woollen textiles then provided a valuable commodity for both domestic use and trade. In the 3rd millennium BC both zooarchaeological data and the evidence of the texts indicate that there was an increased exploitation of sheep for wool, with specific mention of 'wool sheep', the increase in demand being at least partially fuelled by the dramatic rise in population.

As today, looms were used for weaving, and although the looms themselves do not survive, evidence for textile production in the form of clay spindle whorls (for spinning thread) and loom weights (for weighing down the thread) is often found. At Ziyaret Tepe we found many of these, primarily in domestic contexts such as houses and courtyards. Additionally, in the cremation burials we found actual pieces of linen textile, presumed to be the remains of either the clothing or the shrouds of the dead.

Above
A flock scene, from a relief of Tiglath-pileser III
Right
Fragment of textile recovered from a cremation burial

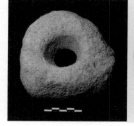

Left Loom weights – these examples made of stone – have been used for weighing down yarn in the weaving process for thousands of years

Above
The annual cotton
harvest

Right
Cleaning wool in the
field

Archaeobotany
Farming and food production

Archaeobotany is the study of human plant use in the past. Most widely, archaeobotany provides information on the plants that made up ancient human diets and economies.

Archaeobotanists are particularly interested in discovering what crops people grew, in order to learn which cereals, legumes, vegetables, fruits, nuts, oils and spices communities used for their food and drinks, the reeds and grasses they used for basket-making, and the plant dyes and fibres used for textile production. But archaeobotany is also able to help archaeologists understand what the environment was like in the past, including reconstructions of vegetation and climate. If we know which plants grew in and around ancient sites, then we can also confirm what the seasonal temperatures must have been like, how much rainfall there would have been, and what kinds of animals could be supported by the landscape. Archaeobotany is also able to help archaeologists learn how agriculture and pastoralism were practised in the past.

There are multiple archaeobotanical methods for studying ancient plant remains. At Ziyaret Tepe, archaeobotanical research focused on analysing the charred remains of ancient seeds that were recovered by collecting soil samples during excavation. Seeds can be preserved in the archaeological record if they have been carbonised, as with wood charcoal. Luckily for archaeobotanists, fire was a regular element of ancient life in communities such as Tušhan, purposefully used for light, heat and cooking in many buildings and open spaces. House fires caused by accident or warfare were also common elements of settled life in the past, and Ziyaret Tepe was no exception. Soil samples were therefore regularly collected from domestic contexts, fire installations and destruction debris in the hope of recovering charred seed remains.

In order to separate the carbonised seeds from the soil they were collected in, each of the archaeobotanical samples at Ziyaret Tepe was put through a flotation machine designed to make plant remains float to the surface of a water tank, where they could then be skimmed off into a sieve, dried and analysed under a microscope for identification. Some seeds, such as olive pits, grape pips and cereal grains, are visible to the naked eye. But many of the plant remains recovered from archaeological samples consist of tiny seeds, 2mm or smaller, that can only be recognised using a stereoscopic microscope.

At Ziyaret Tepe we find a typical assortment of ancient Near Eastern crops: barley, wheat, lentils, peas, vetches, grapes and figs. These foodstuffs would have been produced by farms throughout the fertile lands of the upper Tigris River valley, and brought to Ziyaret Tepe as taxes to be redistributed by the Assyrian state. There is very little archaeobotanical evidence for vegetables, but we can presume that people grew onions, garlic, leeks and salad greens in their home gardens to supplement their meals. One hoard of safflower was discovered in the Bronze Palace on the acropolis: this safflower could both have been used as a

Left
In the course of our time at Ziyaret Tepe the wheat fields surrounding the site (inset) were increasingly replaced by cotton cultivation (main image)

Left
Archaeobotanist Melissa Rosenzweig uses the binocular microscope

Right, top to bottom
Clay animal figurines; archaeozoologist Tina Greenfield works on the collection of ancient animal bones; scene from a relief showing food preparation in a camp

Left and below, top to bottom
Seeds of grape, barley and lentil

flavouring oil and processed into a red dye for textile production. There is no evidence at Ziyaret Tepe for the presence of flax, which could have been used to produce linen. In lieu of flax-based linen, the people of Ziyaret Tepe must have relied on sheep's wool to create cloth. Although sesame is mentioned in Assyrian texts, only a few seeds were found at Ziyaret Tepe, so it appears that sesame oil did not feature prominently in the cuisine of the inhabitants.

Agriculture at Ziyaret Tepe would have relied on the winter rains to water the crops. Fields of cereals and legumes would have been planted in the fall and harvested the following spring. It is possible that the Assyrians at Tušhan built irrigation canals to inundate the fields with water from the Tigris River, although no conclusive evidence for irrigation has been discovered at the site. In the summer shepherds would have herded their sheep, goats and cattle into the higher and cooler foothills surrounding the river valley, where they could graze on the clovers, grasses and shrubs of the steppe. In the winter the animals would have been stabled at Ziyaret Tepe and fed fodder from stocks of barley and legumes.

Zooarchaeology
Reading the bones

Zooarchaeology (or archaeo-zoology!) is the study of animal bones from archaeological sites. Animal remains are key data for understanding the social and economic organisation of early societies because they are the residues of economic behaviour patterns.

The core of zooarchaeology is the analysis of the animal bones recovered in excavation. In addition to identifying which species of animals are represented, which body parts, and the age and sex of specimens, the data can be interrogated for what it can tell us about the patterns of production, butchery, distribution, consumption and disposal of animals. This can shed light on a range of issues relating to the economy, dietary demographics, social status and social organisation, and access to resources and market systems – the tiered exploitational strategies of settlements, cities and empires.

At Ziyaret Tepe, excavations uncovered huge numbers of animal bones from a wide range of contexts from elite and non-elite areas. The animal economy of Tušhan was principally based on the herding of domestic species, and the most frequent animals found, common to all classes, are sheep and goat, followed by cattle and domestic pig. But social differences emerge among the remaining components of the diet. Up in the palace, the elite dined upon choicer cuts of meat and there is evidence for the consumption of high-status wild animals such as deer and boar as well as exotic birds and fish. The lower echelons, by contrast, supplemented their diet with small deer, hare, tortoise and frog.

Decorative ivory

Ivory boxes and tools, furniture decorated with ivory, and unworked elephant tusks were all part of the mass of materials taken by the Assyrians as booty from conquered territories and as tribute from their vassals. Much of this ended up in the magazines of the royal capitals, and excavations at Nimrud in particular have uncovered large quantities of lavishly decorated ivories – furniture elements and toiletry objects, gilded and inlaid with colourful glass or stones, in Levantine and Syrian style. Although evidently available to Assyrian craftsmen, ivory was only rarely employed for Assyrian objects. More common for utilitarian objects such as needles, spindle-whorls and handles, as well as for inlays, was the use of bone, which was, of course, more widely available, although more brittle and less easy to carve.

At Ziyaret Tepe it was a great surprise to come across the finds of decorative rectangular inlays of ivory, ivory cosmetic tubes and an ivory bird-shaped box, as well as small ivory animal figurines that must have been attached to wooden furniture or tools – all discovered in the cremation burials of the governor's palace. The rectangular plaque with musicians displays a very peculiar design that has no parallel in Assyrian art up to now. The ivory rosettes found together with similar bronze rosettes were very likely fixed to a wooden object in an alternating pattern. This use of multiple materials is typical for Near Eastern craftsmanship, contributing to the attractive and precious appearance of these objets d'art.

ZT 0 9 4
ZT 2 9 6 1 5
UYGULAMA SONRASI

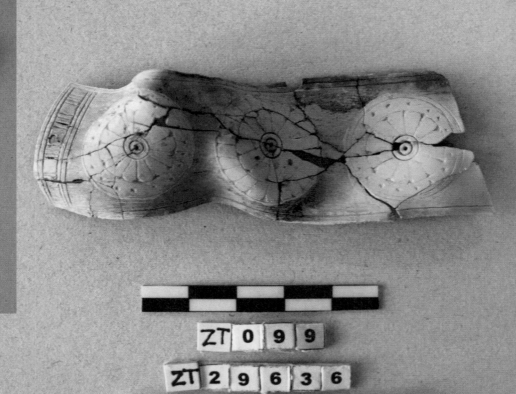

ZT 0 9 9

ZT 2 9 6 3 6

UYGULAMA SONRASI

Above left
Rectangular ivory inlay showing seated musicians playing flute and drums

Left
Fragmented ivory dish with a handle in the shape of an eagle's head

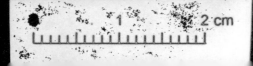

Above
Ivory inlay strip with rosette deign

Left
Furniture attachment in the shape of a resting deer

Reading the ceramics

The most ubiquitous artefacts found on Near Eastern archaeological sites are sherds of ancient pottery. This cheap and easily made commodity has been widely utilised for cooking, serving food and storage for over 8,000 years. Unlike organic materials such as cloth and leather, or metals such as bronze and iron, which suffer from serious decomposition when buried underground, fired clay is remarkably stable and can survive thousands of years in an archaeological deposit.

At Ziyaret Tepe we recovered well over a million potsherds during our excavations. In addition to all of these broken sherds, we found perhaps 200 complete or nearly complete ceramic vessels: bowls, jugs and jars. However, the vast bulk of the material comes not from complete pots, but from fragmentary potsherds. Processing all this data was a Herculean task that involved a team of specialists over the course of the entire project.

What can we learn from all this material? Firstly, for archaeologists ceramics represent a very important source of information for dating. Just as modern clothing fashions change from year to year, so too did the pottery of antiquity. In the course of time the treatment of the clay, the repertoire of forms and the decoration applied all evolved, giving each period its own ceramic signature. While some of these differences can be very subtle, even an untrained eye can rapidly distinguish the

Right
The peace and quiet of the 'sherd garden', behind the dig-house

differences between, say, Nuzi goblets, Assyrian palace ware, painted Cilician bowls, Roman strap-handled jars and medieval glazed pottery. Working from the mass of data coming in from the field, archaeological ceramicists – the specialists who study ancient pottery – create intricate typologies which we can then use for dating archaeological deposits. For example, a pottery vessel smashed on a floor can be used to date an entire building, or a site itself can be dated based on the pottery sherds found on the surface.

At Ziyaret Tepe, while we had a good idea of the overall range of shapes and decorations that the Assyrian potters used, we needed to develop a detailed understanding of how these types changed throughout the nearly three centuries of the Neo-Assyrian period. In order to answer this we constructed a special database designed to record the ceramic inventory, with details of the characteristics, quantity and percentages of each type found in each layer from across the site and from all periods.

As each bucket of pottery was brought in from the field, it came with a coloured tag to denote the importance of the context in which it was found – green for the stratigraphically most important primary contexts, such as floors, pits and burials; yellow for secondary contexts, such as collapsed building materials; and red for tertiary contexts, such as the plough zone and slope wash, which have no stratigraphic meaning, although the material is still of interest.

Depending on the tag, the pottery bucket was treated to a greater or lesser intensity of recording. In general, the pottery was washed each morning and laid out to dry each day in the 'sherd garden'. We would then sort the sherds into distinctive groups based on their 'fabric' (the type of clay and any additions, known as 'temper', such as grit or straw), shape and decoration. These groups of sherds

were then counted, weighed and recorded on forms for subsequent entering into the database for analysis. Over 303,000 of the sherds collected were recorded in this way. A selection of these sherds was then drawn and photographed for further study and for publication.

The end product is the ability to reconstruct the assemblages for each period, to map the distribution of forms across the site down to a room-by-room basis, to make systematic observations on the introduction of new types and the disappearance of old types, and so on.

The Ziyaret Tepe database is one of the largest and most comprehensive databases of Assyrian pottery in existence. This kind of work is slow and painstaking, but in creating an analytical tool which will be of use to our colleagues across the Near East it will make a lasting contribution to the archaeology of the Assyrian Empire.

Below
These polychrome painted sherds are probably of Cilician origin and were recovered buried carefully below the pavement of the floor in the Bronze Palace

Left
Bags of sherds sorted by ware type: part of our research 'library'

Left
Mandy Reimann (left) and Friederike Moll-Dau (right) work on repairing a very large pithos storage jar. Despite using a number of supports, the fabric of the ancient vessel was weak and could not be easily repaired

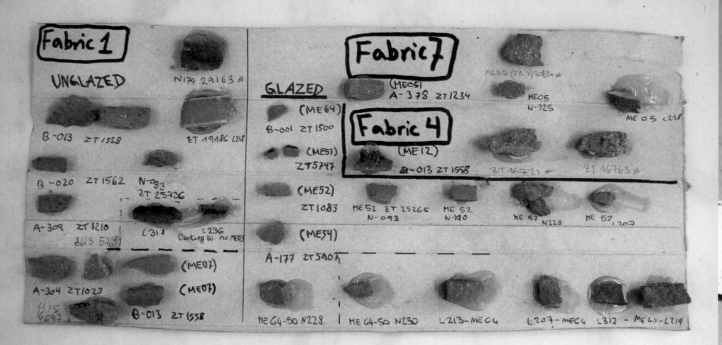

Top
Chart showing
ceramic fabric
types

Above
Helen McDonald assessing
pottery fabric using a
Munsell colour chart

Above, left to right
Barbara Jakubowska, Dr Ania Wodzinska, Natalia Kadzidłowska (nearest to camera) and Agnieszka Poniewierska

Above
Azer Keskin working on recording ceramics

Top
Typical undiagnostic sherds

Ceramic discs

Above left
A typical worked pottery disc

Above right
A rather large disc, this one of glazed pottery, medieval in date

Right
Ceramic 'thin sections': ultra-thin slices of ceramic vessels used to study the composition of the fabric

Right
The storage depot: home to hundreds of crates of ceramics collected over the course of the expedition

Among the large quantities of broken sherds of pottery excavated from the site were sherds that had clearly been worked by human hands, turning them from merely discarded bits of pottery into functional tools. These small sherds are roughly circular, although quite irregular at times. Their sharp edges have been smoothed down. Some have a perforation through the middle while others have only a rough divot where the perforation might have been. Their use remains a mystery. Were these perforated discs simple scrapers, used perhaps for working animal hides into leather? Were they game pieces? Were they convenient weights to hold the warp threads on a hanging loom, or did they serve to prop up furniture on the naturally uneven dirt floors of the houses? Perhaps intense study of these objects, collected in large quantities at Ziyaret Tepe, will one day reveal their intended purpose.

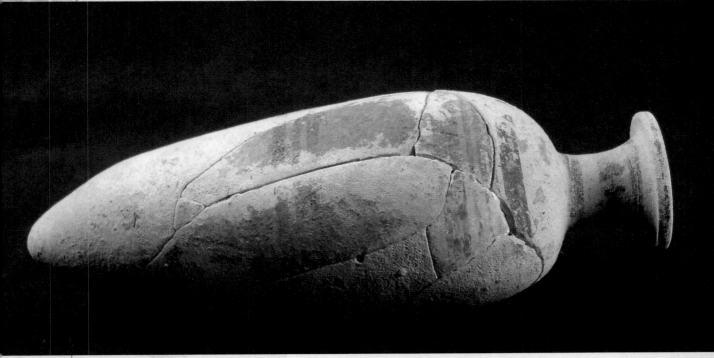

Above
Assyrian
painted bottle
of a type
sometimes
called 'carrot-
shaped'. Our
example is
paralleled by a
similar vessel
found at Nimrud
in the imperial
heartland

Right
Fragment of a
Nuzi-ware
goblet from the
mid-2nd
millennium BC

The working of iron in the Middle Iron Age

The time of the Neo-Assyrian Empire (9th–7th centuries BC) is defined in archaeological terms as the Middle Iron Age. The term Iron Age has been a part of archaeological parlance since its introduction in 1836 by the Danish archaeologist Christian Jürgensen Thomsen, who used the increasing complexity of tool manufacture to classify ancient societies as Stone Age, Bronze Age and Iron Age. Though the details of Thomsen's terminology have changed over the past 180 years, scholars still recognise the importance of iron as a transformative material for ancient societies.

The properties of iron that make it a superior material for tools are well known: it is harder, stronger and holds a cutting edge better than the copper and bronze it replaced. Likewise, raw iron ore is far more common and widespread than the deposits of copper ore and tin across the Near East. Iron, however, requires higher temperatures to smelt the ore and work the metal, and the introduction of carbon to produce the fine-edged tools we associate with iron today. Copper and bronze are typically cast into moulds while in a liquid state. In the ancient Near East, however, iron was worked in a solid state. The technology used for producing objects in iron is very different from that used for other metals.

Iron metallurgy predates the beginning of the Iron Age, with its earliest use occurring during the Early Bronze Age (3rd millennium BC). So the Assyrian smiths were using a technology for the production of their tools and weapons which was already ancient. At Ziyaret Tepe we have no direct evidence of iron smithing during the Assyrian period. Typically, one might expect to find evidence of kilns or forges, iron-working tools or at least slag, the waste product formed when ore is smelted. While the excavations did in fact recover a large amount of slag, we are still in the process of analysing what type, or types, of slag these are – whether from ironworking, copper or bronze metallurgy, or the manufacture of pottery or glass.

What we do have evidence for is the use of iron artefacts. Many of these are weapons used by the Assyrian army which would have been garrisoned at Tušhan. Knives, arrowheads and scale armour made of iron have all been recovered. Another common find is fibulae (brooches) – while the majority we found were made of bronze, we also have examples in iron. In the fibula illustrated below, the pin is attached at the bow (body) with a spring that creates tension to hold it in place.

Left A simple iron ring

Right Iron and copper nails

Below Iron fibula

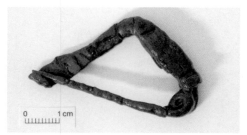

The humble nail

If any single thing holds society together, surely it is the nail. Small but sharp, this unassuming accessory has been fastening objects little and large with quiet dedication for a very long time.

The first nails were made of copper over 5,000 years ago. At Ziyaret Tepe we found nails of iron in all major periods of occupation – from the Roman levels in particular they were a very common find.

ZT8063
A 923

Top
A blacksmith's
workshop in
Diyarbakır

Left
Copper dagger,
iron knife
and copper
spearhead

Above
Scales of
Assyrian armour

Copper
and bronze

Some of the world's earliest evidence for the use of copper comes from southeastern Anatolia, where beads and small tools are found in small quantities at a number of Neolithic settlements. Even today, copper working remains a vibrant tradition in Turkish cities, including Diyarbakır.

Copper is found in small quantities as native copper, but as copper ore it is widely distributed across the Near East, being found in Cyprus, Turkey, Israel, Jordan and Iran. Copper has a relatively low melting point and can easily be worked into a variety of ornaments, vessels and tools. There is, however, a problem with these: the metal is too soft to hold a working edge for long, and tools made of copper need to be constantly resharpened.

This problem was solved in ancient times by the addition of other elements which improved the workability of the copper, creating the first alloys. The two principal alloys were arsenic and tin which, when alloyed with copper, make what we call bronze. Arsenical bronze and tin bronze were both widely used in the Chalcolithic period (roughly the 4th millennium BC), but by the Neo-Assyrian period the predominant alloy was of copper and tin.

Bronze has several advantages over copper as a material. Not only does it keep a sharp edge for longer, but it is also easier to cast than pure copper,

Above
Bronze button

Below
Dr Latif Özen analyses the composition of metal artefacts using X-ray fluorescence spectroscopy

making it an excellent choice for small, detailed artefacts such as arrowheads for hunting and warfare, or ornaments such as bells and buttons. Some of the most common bronze artefacts found during the Ziyaret Tepe excavations were fibulae.

Bronze is, however, not usually found in large quantities on archaeological sites, for several reasons. Firstly, under many conditions the material does not preserve well. It is susceptible to decay in moist environments and artefacts are frequently found suffering from what conservators call 'bronze rot disease', which occurs when copper or bronze comes into contact with chloride salts in the soil. Secondly, most bronze artefacts in antiquity were recycled when they became unusable. Unlike pottery and stone, when a bronze artefact breaks, it can be melted down and recast. In fact, hoards of scrap metal were a valuable commodity, collected and traded over long distances.

The one type of context at Ziyaret Tepe where we did find significant quantities of bronze was in the cremation burials. However, in Assyrian times bronze was a luxury item and in the lower-status households of the period artefacts of bronze are much less common.

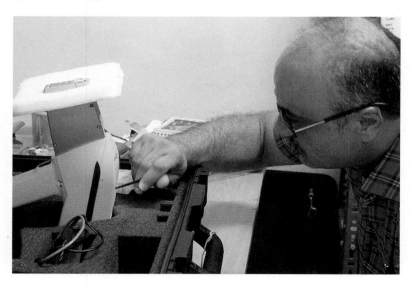

Above
A coppersmith
in Diyarbakır

Right
A typical Iron Age
trilobate (three-
bladed) arrowhead

0   1 cm

Jewellery

The desire to decorate oneself is as old as humankind. The earliest depictions of humans show designs directly painted onto the body or applied as tattoos or decorative scars. Wearing ornaments – whether on the feet, hands, arms or, above all, the head – was a practice common to all, rich and poor.

Depending on their economic status and taste there was, of course, a great discrepancy as to the materials used. Gold jewellery – in particular when combined with colourful rare stones – was restricted to the rich upper classes. In any case, in antiquity wearing jewellery was not the prerogative of women. Whereas women obviously took pride in elaborate earrings and head-decorations such as diadems and simple headbands, men also wore necklaces and rings, as well as bracelets and armlets, which might be awarded as a mark of royal favour. The terminals of these were often shaped into animal heads, most often in the form of gazelles, snakes or lions. A common find are simple crescent-shaped earrings with a number of droplets at the end. Pins for fixing items of clothing in place might be plain or crafted with complicated, decorative pinheads. Longer pins with stronger shafts could be used as hairpins or to hold veils in place. All this is evidenced both in depictions in sculptures and wall paintings and, more especially, from finds in graves, where personal jewellery was often deposited with the dead for their use in the afterlife. Besides fulfilling a decorative function, the motifs and patterns embellished on jewellery also often had a symbolic

Opposite page
A selection of jewellery of different materials and periods. Clockwise from top left: bronze earring; carnelian pendant; bronze hairpin; gold rosette, possibly from a necklace

Below
Bronze torque bracelet

meaning, mostly to protect the owner from evil spirits.

Gold always remained the most highly prized material. But bronze can also take on a glimmering sheen and appear golden when polished, so it is perhaps not surprising that bronze jewellery items were in fact the most numerous finds we came across in the excavations. Lastly, even iron might be used for some items, especially for fibulae (brooches) for fastening cloaks. In a few instances metals were combined, as with a twisted bronze and silver ring from the palace. In the later Hellenistic and Roman periods, glass and bronze were employed to imitate gold and semi-precious stones. In the Islamic period the use of jewellery made of glass, in particular rings, bracelets and pendants, was very popular. By then, the working of glass had been perfected and allowed the production of elaborate, colourful objects.

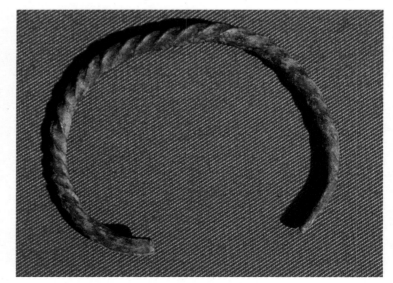

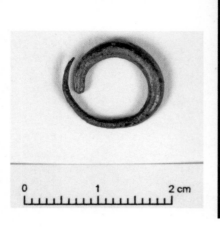

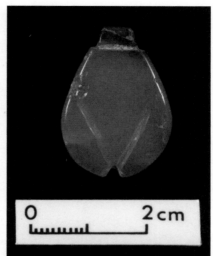

0 ‖⊥⊥⊥⊥⊥⊥‖ 2 cm

ZT 19037
L 205

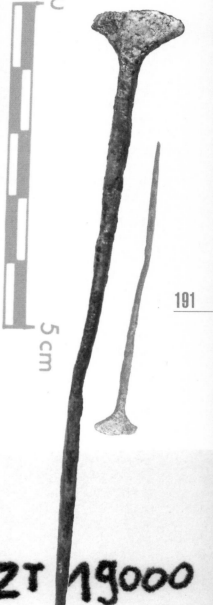

ZT 19000
L-201

ZT 19000
L-201

0 ⊥⊥⊥⊥⊥⊥⊥⊥⊥⊥ 1 ⊥⊥⊥⊥⊥⊥⊥⊥⊥⊥ 2 cm

Ground stone

Ground stone is typically used for utilitarian tools and Ziyaret Tepe is no exception. The most common tool, the grinding stone, comes in sets of two pieces, one held in the hand (the handstone) and the bottom stationary piece (the grinding stone). These tools for grinding grain are found in nearly the same shape and size from the Middle Bronze Age through to the medieval period, a span of 3,000 years. They make up almost a quarter of all the ground stone artefacts found at the site. Besides grinding stones, other ground stone tools such as mortars, pestles and various pounders were used for food preparation. Along with features such as hearths, these tools help in identifying areas where food was prepared.

Pounding and abrading tools may also have been used to grind pigments or medicines. Other uses for ground stone include in construction, as door sockets and architectural decorations. At a much smaller scale, stone beads account for a quarter of all the stone objects found from the Late Assyrian period (see separate section ahead on beads).

The ground stone industry diversified during the Bronze and Iron Ages, as growing cities created new demands for prestige goods. The elite in Tušhan used stone vessels to show off their wealth, possibly preferring stone for the very features that pottery lacks: translucency, shine, durability and the high cost of manufacture. Elaborate stone objects – perhaps artefacts of high-status gift-exchange – are found both in the palace and in private houses, and in graves as well as in domestic contexts. One beautiful,

highly polished stone vessel from the cremation burials had been fragmented into many pieces by the burning. Another vessel, also from a cremation burial, had only been broken into two pieces. Some of these elite stone vessels copy the shape of Late Assyrian palace-ware pottery forms, but in a more durable and costly material. Others made of alabaster or calcite copy shapes typical of jars found in Egypt.

Top
Grinding stones such as this one, broken in half, are very common in the Middle East

Above
This fine stone bowl is rare and closely imitates pottery forms

Above
A highly
polished stone
dish, burnt in
a cremation
burial

Below
Utilitarian stone
tools include a
handstone (left),
mortar (centre)
and pestle (right)

Chipped stone

Top
Alabaster jar from a cremation burial

Below
Monumental door socket from Room 7 of the palace

Humans have been chipping or flaking stone into shape for thousands of years. Such basic technology was especially important before metals were widely used. Even with the advent of bronze and then iron tools, however, chipped stone was still used for some purposes because of its durability, ease of manufacture and low cost. Nevertheless, a steady decline in the use of chipped stone can be seen over time.

Most of the stone found at Ziyaret Tepe dates to the medieval and Late Assyrian periods – of the total 12,225 pieces of chipped stone found, 45% are from Late Assyrian contexts and 14% are from medieval ones.

Commonly used raw materials include flint, quartz and, occasionally, obsidian. The Early Bronze Age levels at the site contain large, specially made flint blades with sickle gloss: these were used for harvesting grain. In the Late Assyrian period, common tools include less-elaborate items such as notched flakes, retouched flakes and side scrapers, along with 'debitage' – debris indicating locations where chipped stone tools were produced. By the medieval period, formally shaped tools declined in number and the main tools became retouched and notched flakes.

One of the more unusual types found in the Late Assyrian period were tiny projectile points, most under 2cm long. Many were found in Operation A/N and their size suggests they may have been used for hunting birds or small game – perhaps a favourite pastime of the elite.

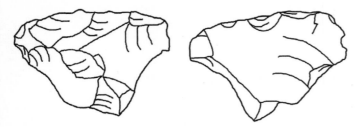

Left Drawing of an Assyrian chipped flint blade tool

Below Chipped stone pieces include this flint ball (top), perhaps used as a drain stopper, and a polished flint sickle from the Early Bronze Age (below)

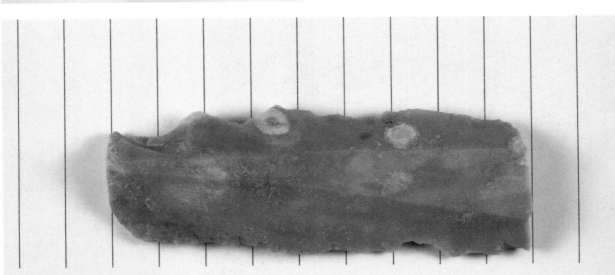

5 CM

Sweeping the floors

Preceding page
The herds of Tepe move through the morning dust

Main picture
Britt Hartenberger sorting microdebris

Below
Bronze pin and earring and (left) and microbeads (right)

Microdebris consists of tiny fragments of artefacts that have been lost and ended up in corners, between floorboards or embedded in floors. For certain activities, if people did not discard items where they used them, utilised materials that disintegrate, or took artefacts with them when they left, the microdebris can provide the only evidence that these activities took place. It can help with the identification of room function – in buildings such as those of Operation G/R built-in features such as hearths and artefacts left in place provide some clues, but analysis of the microdebris can add to this, even showing that multiple activities took place in some areas.

Room 3, for example, had bones and fine pottery, but no cooking wares or other cooking features, suggesting that food was consumed but not prepared here. A concentration of chipped stone debris was found in the northeast corner of the room, indicating that stone tool manufacture may have taken place here as well. In Room 7 a concentration of tiny bones, pottery fragments and lithic fragments at its north end suggests that craft production may have been carried out.

Another benefit of studying microdebris is finding objects that are invisible at a larger scale, such as microbeads, fragments of metal and the tiny bones of smaller animals, most of which would be missed in standard excavation procedures. It is the microdebris evidence that shows that small mammals, birds and fish were part of the diet at Tušhan. We

Right
Bones collected
via microdebris
analysis.
Every find was
accompanied by
a ZT tag

even know that there were rodents living in the drains. To give another example, tiny shards of glass found in medieval microdebris demonstrate that glass vessels had been used, even though these fragile objects were not actually found in the excavations.

Above and right
The tedious sorting of microdebris can result in finds such as this fragment of a cuneiform tablet

Beads

Above
`The excavations produced a panoply of beads, in many materials: here steatite, carnelian, limestone and frit`

A
s in modern days, beads were utilised as decorative elements to enhance the beauty and attractiveness of the person. Therefore beads needed to be made of colourful materials in order to give a contrast to the otherwise rather dull or plain-coloured clothes and textiles worn in ancient times. Intensely coloured stones, such as the dark-blue lapis lazuli or the bright-orange carnelian,

were strongly favoured through all times, as was the multi-coloured agate, which was often shaped into eye-stones. These stones had to be imported from far away – from Afghanistan or Southern Iran – and were comparatively expensive and rare. More common local stones were also used, such as the dark-green steatite, which could take on an attractive and shiny appearance once polished.

Easier to manufacture were beads of glass and frit, a silicious, artificial material similar to glass, though not translucent. The larger spherical Assyrian glass beads were mostly of light-blue colour; a multi-coloured bead with dot-and-circle decoration in the famous millefiori technique resembles the blue and white glass beads still popular throughout the Near and Middle East. In fact, many beads discovered in Ziyaret Tepe were tiny: smaller than 1mm in size, difficult to spot

Left
`Agate 'eye-stone' bead`

ZT 15612
G-406

Left
Bead made of
black and white
glass

Far left
Black and white
millefiore bead,
probably
medieval
Left Blue and
white millefiore
bead from the
medieval layers
in Operation L

in the earth and often recovered in
screening. They may have been used to
decorate garments or shawls.

Throughout all periods in the ancient
Near East, beads were often shaped into
petals or floral elements in order to imitate
flowers. Other shapes, common to all
periods even until today, are spherical,
lentoid or elongated forms for stringing
into bracelets and necklaces. With the help
of multi-perforated spacer beads, several
strands of beads could form a splendid
necklace, something even depicted in
Assyrian reliefs and on terracotta figurines.

One aspect with regard to the material
and colour of beads was their magical
connotations. As in parts of the world
even today, stones and colours were
associated with gods and attributed
magical properties. As such, certain beads
were believed to ward off evil or attract the
love of another person.

Above Dirk Wicke (in the hat) consults with two of our conservators, Charlotte Rérolle and Yvonne Helmholz, about how best to stabilise the fragile surface of a fallen piece of painted Assyrian wall plaster in the Bronze Palace

Chapter 5
Conservation and communication

Diyarbakır Museum

Most of our conservation efforts took place at the dig-house or in the field. Occasionally, however, we recovered artefacts that required greater time and resources than we could devote at the dig-house and, with the generous co-operation of the director of the Diyarbakır Museum and our *temsilci* (government representative), our conservators were able to work in the museum on especially large or difficult pieces.

One of the most spectacular finds we made at Ziyaret Tepe was a fragment of an Assyrian wall painting that once decorated the interior of the Bronze Palace. The wall plaster had fallen during the collapse of the building, but remarkably a few large pieces had survived in the rubble for two-and-a-half thousand years, until uncovered by Dr Wicke and his team.

Most people are familiar with the famous bas-reliefs found in the middle of the 19th century at the great Assyrian imperial capitals of Nineveh, Nimrud and Khorsabad. These iconic images are carved in low relief on stone slabs and lined the corridors and rooms of the royal palaces.

In the peripheries of the Empire the palaces were still ornate, but less expensively decorated. Instead of stone orthostats, the Assyrian artisans made elaborate polychrome paintings on white plaster, often following the same kinds of imagery seen in sculptures in the imperial heartland.

After the discovery of fallen wall paintings at Ziyaret Tepe, Dr Wicke consulted with our conservators, Yvonne Helmholz and Charlotte Rérolle, on how best to proceed with the excavation, cleaning and conservation. It was decided that it needed to be lifted *en bloc* and transported to the museum for conservation.

First the archaeologists excavated beneath the plaster, leaving the delicate painted surface on a pedestal of mud brick. Next the plaster itself was covered in plastic film and its sides covered in aluminium foil. After that, bandages soaked in wet plaster were put around the edges to create a hard shell that would physically support the plaster. Then the top was covered in plaster, creating what we called the 'egg'. It was very heavy, and for transporting to the museum we built robust wooden boxes. One of our eggs was so large that getting it inside required removing the museum doors! Of course, we also brought along all the

The recovery of an Assyrian wall painting, from lifting the block of earth on site through to being ready for display

smaller pieces to see if we could fit them back together.

Once it was inside the museum, three of our conservators spent months cleaning, stabilising and consolidating the wall painting. On the previous page, Lourdes Mesa García, Yvonne Helmholz and Olga Emgrund can be seen cleaning the paintings during the 2014 season. The top cover of plaster has been removed and Yvonne is blowing away dust using an air syringe. Work proceeds with the use of small paint brushes, scalpels and pointed wooden sticks. Slowly the details of the painted plaster are revealed. The finished product shows details of the extraordinary Assyrian craftsmanship.

While the wall plaster was undoubtedly our most involved conservation project,

our team also worked on the artefacts which are now permanent parts of the Diyarbakır Museum display and study collections. But the work of the conservator is never done. Even after the initial cleaning and stabilisation, the artefacts continue to require attention and conservation treatment. In the image above, Friederike Moll-Dau cleans a bronze bowl from Ziyaret Tepe that was taken to the museum in a past season but requires additional conservation work. With care, these artefacts will remain a part of Turkey's rich cultural heritage for many generations to come.

Above
Friederike Moll-Dau works on cleaning a bronze bowl

Right
Lourdes Mesa García inspects glass fragments through an illuminated magnifying glass

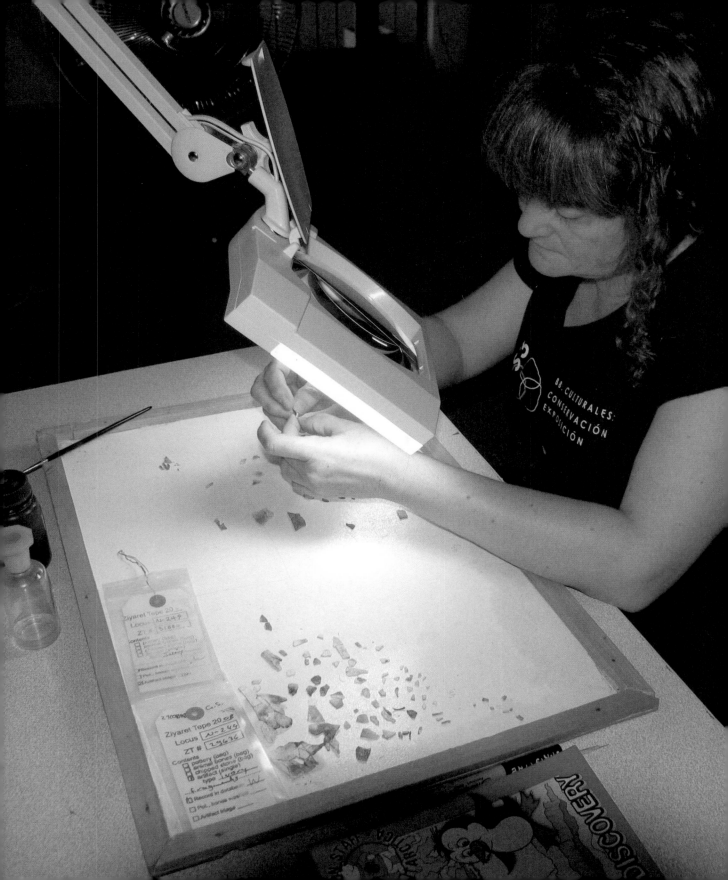

Communicating the excavation results

Left
Prof. Dr
Kemalettin
Köroğlu gives
an evening
lecture to
the villagers
in Tepe on
the finds from
their ancient
mound

Communicating results is critical to the work of the archaeologist. Without publication the information would be lost and years of careful excavation wasted. But we have always wanted as many people as possible to know about this amazing project, and throughout we have been at pains to communicate our results to the widest possible audience.

At the heart of this, of course, are the scientific contributions. Preliminary reports are published in the international journal *Anatolica*, giving an overview of each season's work and the principal findings. These are supplemented by the work of the individual specialists, with articles in a very wide range of scientific journals on the archaeo-environmental datasets, the geophysical results, epigraphic finds, and subsets of the material culture such as lithics, ivory, tokens and seals.

In all, the project has already published more than 100 scientific papers, with more in the pipeline. These will in turn feed into the final reports, a multi-volume series which will be the definitive publication of the excavations. Many team members have given lectures to universities and to the general public in their home countries and across the world. This has been accompanied by press releases and coverage in all major media. To give one example, the tablet from the palace with the mysterious names caused a sensation, making it into global news on radio, television and the press: it was hailed by *Time* magazine as one of its top 100 scientific discoveries of the year, and even made it into a children's newspaper in Hong Kong! More locally, at the end of the project our senior Turkish collaborator, Prof. Kemalettin Köroğlu, gave a lecture on our work to the Tepe villagers. Well over 100 people, including the mayor, our workmen, their families and the children of Tepe attended. A projector was set up using the outside wall of one of the village teahouses, helping to provide a perfect evening to explain our work and to thank the villagers for their support over our two decades in Tepe.

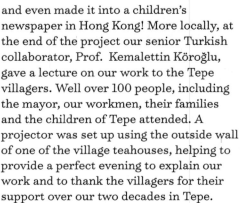
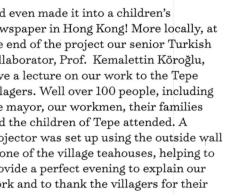

ANATOLICA XXIX, 2003

ARCHAEOLOGICAL INVESTIGATIONS AT ZIYARET TEPE – 2002

Timothy Matney, John MacGinnis, Helen McDonald, Kathleen Nicoll, Lynn Rainville, Michael Roaf, Monica L. Smith and Diana Stein

ANATOLICA XXXI, 2005

ARCHAEOLOGICAL INVESTIGATIONS AT ZIYARET TEPE 2003 – 2004

Timothy Matney and Lynn Rainville (editors) with contributions from Timothy Demko, Sara Kayser, Kemalettin Köroğlu, Helen McDonald, John MacGinnis, Kathleen Nicoll, Simo Parpola, Mandy Reimann, Michael Roaf, Philipp Schmidt, and Jeffrey Szuchman

ANATOLICA XXXIII, 2007

REPORT ON EXCAVATIONS AT ZIYARET TEPE, 2006 SEASON

Timothy Matney, Lynn Rainville, Kemalettin Köroğlu, Azer Keskin, Tasha Vorderstrasse, Nursen Özkul Fındık, and Ann Donkin

ANATOLICA XXXV, 2009

EXCAVATIONS AT ZIYARET TEPE 2007-2008

Timothy Matney, Tina Greenfield, Britt Hartenberger, Azer Keskin, Kemalettin Köroğlu, John MacGinnis, Willis Monroe, Lynn Rainville, Mary Shepperson, Tasha Vorderstrasse, and Dirk Wicke

ANATOLICA XXXVII, 2011

EXCAVATIONS AT ZIYARET TEPE, DIYARBAKIR PROVINCE, TURKEY, 2009-2010 SEASONS

Timothy Matney, Tina Greenfield, Britt Hartenberger, Chelsea Jalbrzikowski, Kemalettin Köroğlu, John MacGinnis, Anke Marsh, Martin Willis Monroe, Melissa Rosenzweig, Kristina Sauer, and Dirk Wicke

Tuesday 26th June, 2012 n° 2194

www.daily10online.com

DAILY 10

Read English for 15 minutes each day

Email your art to editor@daily7-daily10 with your name, age, details and a photo of self. Please write 'Daily Art' in the subject line

Unknown language discovered on ancient tablet

Archaeologists have found a stone tablet with ancient unknown writing...

Mapping the Past: An Archaeogeophysical Case Study from Southeastern Turkey

by Timothy Matney and Ann Donkin

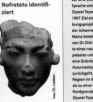

Internationale Nachrichten

Nachrichten aus der Welt der internationalen Archäologie finden Sie auch auf unserer Facebookseite.

ÄGYPTEN

Neuer Kopf der Nofretete identifiziert

Abb. 1 Das Material und die fragmentarisch erhaltene Kopfbedeckung geben Anlass für eine Neuinterpretation des Dargestellten.

Foto: Ch. Loeben.

Christian Loeben, der Ägyptologe des Museums August Kestner in Hannover, hält ein Bildnis, das bislang Pharao Echnaton (1353–1336 v. Chr.) zugeschrieben wurde, für ein Porträt von dessen Gattin Nofretete. Als Gründe für die Neubenennung nannte Loeben das Material – Quarzit sei typisch für Frauenfiguren – und die erhaltenen Reste einer Königinnen-Krone. Das 5,5 cm große Köpfchen ist Teil einer Privatsammlung und wird vom 6.– 10. Juni 2012 auf der Brüsseler Antikenmesse «Brussels Ancient Art Fair» (BAAF), zu sehen sein.

AW-Redaktion

TÜRKEI

Neuassyrischer Text gibt Hinweise auf eine bislang unbekannte Sprache

Bei Ausgrabungen im Südosten der Türkei fanden Archäologen 2009 eine assyrische Tontafel, die Hinweise auf eine bislang nicht identifizierte Sprache enthält (Abb. 1). Der Fundort Ziyaret Tepe am Oberen Tigris ist seit 1997 Ziel eines internationalen Grabungsprojektes, an dem auch ein Team der Johannes Gutenberg-Universität Mainz beteiligt ist. Unter der Leitung von Dr. Dirk Wicke werden die Überreste eines neuassyrischen Gouverneurspalastes untersucht, der vermutlich auf eine Gründung des assyrischen Königs Assurnasirpal II. (883–859 v. Chr.) zurückgeht. Die Assyrer eroberten die Region im 9. Jh. v. Chr. und machten sie zu einer wichtigen Provinz an ihrer Nordgrenze. In dem Ruinenhügel Ziyaret Tepe wird die Hauptstadt der gleichnamigen assyrischen Provinz Tušhan lokalisiert.

Der Keilschrifttext ZTT 30 stammt vermutlich aus dem Archiv des Palastes und enthält eine Liste von 144 Frauen, die in der Verfügungsgewalt der assyrischen Verwaltung standen. Gibt der Text bereits interessante Informationen über die Arbeits- und Aufgabenverteilung in der assyrischen Provinzverwaltung, so erlaubt eine detaillierte Studie der Personennamen weitere Rückschlüsse auf die Zusammensetzung der Bevölkerung. Der Philologe Dr. John MacGinnis vom McDonald Institute for Archaeological Research der University of Cambridge konnte in seiner Arbeit zu dem Text lediglich 15 der erhaltenen 59 Namen als akkadisch, hurritisch, luwisch bzw. altiranisch identifizieren; 44 Namen weisen keinerlei erkennbare Verbindungen zu bekannten altorientalischen Sprachen auf.

Diese Frauen könnten im Zuge der assyrischen Deportationspolitik

Abb. 1 Die Tontafel verzeichnet Namen einer noch nicht erforschten Sprache.

aus anderen Regionen des Reiches nach Tušhan gebracht worden sein. Möglicherweise aber, so MacGinnis, gehörten sie auch einer lokalen Bevölkerung an, die vor den Assyrern in den nordmesopotamischen Regionen ansässig war. Insofern könnte es sich um Angehörige aus dem Volk der Subrier handeln, die bislang kaum fassbar sind. Ebenso sind vor-hurritische oder vor-indoiranische Bevölkerungsteile in Betracht zu ziehen, die aus den Gebieten des Kaukasus oder Zagros stammen könnten, Regionen, die für ihre Sprachvielfalt bekannt sind. Eine weitere Möglichkeit ist es, in den nicht etymologisierbaren Namen Frauen aus dem Volk der Muški (Phryger) zu sehen, welches im ausgehenden 2. Jt. v. Chr. nach Anatolien einwanderte.

Dr. Dirk Wicke

Link zur Homepage des Ziyaret Tepe Archaeological Project:
http://www3.uakron.edu/ziyaret/.

ARCHAEOLOGY

THE COSMOS

TIME

100 New Scientific Discoveries

Fascinating, Momentous, and Mind-Expanding Stories

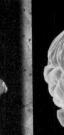

EARTH

THE MIND

DISPLAY UNTIL 4/5/13
$12.99US $16.99CAN

---

12 23 Ağustos 2000 Çarşamba DİYARBA

Güneydoğu'nun Cano'

Selim KAYA/ Faruk YÜCE

DİYARBAKIR - Kültür Bakanı İstemihan Talay, baraj alanı olarak belirlenen toprakların altında ve üstünde kalacak tarihi eserlerin kurtarılması çalışmalarının, "kuyumcu hassasiyetiyle" sürdürülmesi gerektiğini söyledi. Ilısu ve Karkamış Baraj gölleri altında kalacak tarihi eserlerin kurtarılması çerçevesinde Diyarbakır'ın Bismil ve Batman'ın Hasankeyf ilçelerindeki kazı çalışmalarını gözlemek amacıyla beraberinde DSP İstanbul Milletvekili Ahmet Tan ve DSP Diyarbakır Milletvekili A. Samet Turgut ile birlikte Diyarbakır'a gelen Bakan Talay, Valilik Toplantı Salonu'nda bir açıklama yaptı. İl Valisi Ahmet Cemil Serhadlı, günün anlam ve önemini hatırsaz olarak Bakan Talay'a bir plaket sundu. Bakan İstemihan Talay daha sonra beraberindekilerle Valiliğin toplantı salonuna geçti.

Talay burada ilk sözü Ortadoğu Teknik Üniversitesi Öğretim Üyesi Prof. Dr. Numan Tuna'ya verdi. Prof. Dr. Numan Tuna ve Karkamış Baraj Gölleri altında kalacak olan arkeolojik kültür varlıklarını kurtarma projesi çerçevesinde sürdürülen çalışmalarda Zeugma ve Hasankeyf'te önemli bir aşama kaydettiklerini söyledi.

Hasankeyf'teki tarihi güzelliklerin su altında kalmadan bunların bir an önce belgelenmesi gerektiğini sözlerine ekleyen Prof. Dr. Numan Tuna, "Bu çalışmanın asıl sahibi Kültür Bakanlığıdır. Ancak GAP İdaresi ve DSİ'den de büyük destek alıyoruz. Özellikle Zeugma'daki bulgular, tarihi sahiplenme konusunda bizleri bilinçlendirmektedir. Bu tür arkeolojik yerlerin korunması lazım" dedi. Prof. Dr. Tuna, daha sonra su altında kalacak olan arkeolojik noktaları dev ekranda basın mensuplarına gösterdi.

Kültür Bakanı Talay, burada, Bakanlıkça bir süre önce başlatılan Güneydoğu Anadolu Bölgesi'ndeki kültürel varlıkların kurtarılması ve belgelenmesi projesi kapsamında yapılan kazı çalışmalarına Devlet Su İşleri'nin finansal destek verdiğini, ODTÜ Tarihsel Çevre Araştırma Merkezi'nin ise (TAÇDAM) projenin sekreteryalığı görevini üstlendiğini belirtti.

Dünyanın kültür mirasına ve arkeolojik bilimine katkı sağlaması amacıyla da en hızlı ve en kapsamlı çalışmaların Türkiye'de elbirliğiyle yürütüldüğünü belirten Bakan Talay, "Diyarbakır'ın Bismil ve Batman'ın Hasankeyf ilçeleri ile Gaziantep ile Mardin'deki gezimi, belirli bölgelerdeki kurtarma ve belgeleme çalışmalarını yerinde incelemek amacıyla yapacağım. Baraj alanı olarak belirlenen toprakların altında ve üstünde kalacak tarihi eserlerin kurtarılması çalışmaları, bir kuyumcu hassasiyetiyle sürüyor." dedi.

-DÜNYA BANKASIYLA İŞBİRLİĞİ-

Kültür Bakanı Talay, Dünya Bankası ile ortaklaşa olarak tarihi mirasın korunması amacıyla işbirliği başlatıldığını belirterek şöyle devam etti: "Bakanlığımızda, bir koordinatörlük oluşturuldu. Bu koordinatörlükte, Dünya Bankası'nın da finansal destek sağlayacağı hangi

kültür mirasına aday kent olarak gösterdik. Bu arada, Diyarbakır surlarıyla çok büyük önem taşıyan bir şehirimiz. Yine, Diyarbakır'ın dünya kültür mirasına aday kent olarak gösterildik. "

Öte yandan gazetecilerin, Cumhurbaşkanı Ahmet Necdet Sezer'in Hasankeyf'e ilişkin KHK'yi ikinci kez iadesiyle ilgili sorularını Talay, "Ben buraya tarihi eserlerin korunması çalışmalarını incelemek amacıyla geldim" şeklinde cevap verdi. ODTÜ Mimarlık Fakültesi öğretim üyesi ve TAÇDAM Başkanı Prof. Dr. Numan Tuna ise Bakan Talay'a slayt gösterisiyle Ilısu ve Karkamış Baraj gölleri hakkında bilgi verdi.

BAKAN BİSMİL'DE

Diyarbakır'ın Bismil ilçesindeki Ziyaret Tepe bölgesinde baraj Gölü altında kalacak tarihi eserlerin kurtarılması çerçevesinde yürütülen kazı çalışmalarıyla ilgili bilgi alan Bakan Talay, burada yapılan çalışmaların, bu bölgede çalışma yapan ABD'li bilim adamlarının katkılarıyla dünya Türkiye'deki tarihi eserleri gün ışığına çıkarmaya devam ettik. Türkiye Cumhuriyeti Hükümeti'nin, tarihi kültür varlıklarını koruma için çok önemli olduğunu da dile getiren Bakan Talay, şöyle dedi:

Bölgedeki kazı alanlarında çalışan tarihi eserler, tarihi çevre bilimsel kuruluşlara veriliyor. Böylece çalışmalar başlamış olan sonra bu çalışmalar, bilimsel eserlerin dönüşüyor. Yarınlara dünya Türkiye'deki tarihi zenginliklerin korunduğunu görüyoruz. Bu arkeolojik mirasımızı, bakanlığın kayıtlarındadır. Bu bölgedeki kazı çalışmaları, tüm dünya ve ülkemiz için çok önemlidir. Çünkü kültür ve tarih bilincini ortaya koymakta ve bu bilinç de, toplumu bir araya gelmesini sağlamaktadır.

1998 yılında DSİ Genel Müdürlüğü ile yaptığımız toplantılar altında kalan kültür varlıklarının denetiminde ODTÜ ile işbirliğin başmalanı devam etmesi konusunda karar aldık. Daha sonra kalıntılar belgelenmeye başlandı. Bu belgeleme, bizi telaşa hızlı bir biçimde belirli kaynaklarla yapıldı. Bu kazı çalışmaları Dünya Bankası'ndan 50 milyon dolar kredi alacağız."

Kültür Bakanı İstemihan Talay, Zeugma'nın bir kısmının sular altında kaldığını da kaydederek, "Bu bölgede zor çalışmalar yaparak, bazı kalıntıları kurtardık. Zeugma'da çok zengin kalıntılar var. Oradaki çalışmalar ve Zeugma'yı açık müze haline getirme çalışmalarımız sürüyor" dedi.

HASANKEYF

Talay, Hasankeyf ilçesinde Ilısu Baraj Gölü altında kalacak olan tarihi eserlerin kurtarılması çerçevesinde devam eden kazı çalışmalarının yapıldığı Kale Mahallesi'nde incelemelerde bulundu, ardından bilgi aldı. Bakan Talay ve beraberindekiler, Hasankeyf ilçesindeki

---

Cano'da Bakan

▼ Kültür Bakanı İstemihan Talay, Ilısu ve Karkamış baraj gölleri altında kalacak olan arkeolojik kültür varlıklarını kurtarma projesi çerçevesinde Güneydoğu'da sürdürülen kazı çalışmalarını yerinde incelemek üzere dün Diyarbakır'a geldi. **12'DE**

The new museum in Diyarbakır

Towards the very end of our project, a long-term goal of the Turkish government was achieved when renovations undertaken on the old citadel (*kale*) of Diyarbakır, known in antiquity as Amedi, was completed, and a tourist centre for the city was established. One of the principal buildings on the citadel was

Left
Craftsmen working on the reconstruction of a section of the famous Assyrian mosaic pavements

Below
The finished pavement, faithfully recreating the Assyrian original

215

dedicated to a new museum and, after many false starts and a long planning process, the exhibitions came together quickly in the last two years of our project. We were delighted to be informed that artefacts from Ziyaret Tepe would occupy two large rooms on the upper floor of the museum.

The preparations were intense: artefact lists, text panels and the conserved objects themselves were supplemented with video footage showing reconstructions of the major Assyrian buildings, drawings and photographs. Our team donated hundreds of hours of their time to making sure that the display would be a valuable cultural resource for the people of Diyarbakır in the years to come.

One of the more ambitious projects undertaken was the reconstruction of an Assyrian mosaic pavement. We provided the museum with photographs and detailed drawings of the mosaics, and their craftsmen set to work. A large load of white and black river stones was brought to the museum and a frame constructed of cement blocks. Next the workers set the stones in concrete (the original floor was set in mud plaster) in a pattern following the original Assyrian model. The final product was very impressive, and while not quite up to the quality of the Assyrian original, which had much smaller stones, it certainly gives the museum visitor a wonderful visual impression of what the floors at Tušhan would have looked like. Later the museum built a low mud-brick wall and removed the concrete blocks, completing the effect.

The cases were designed specifically with our artefacts in mind and we worked closely with the museum authorities to maximise the use of space and to convey as much information as possible. The text panels and video presentations included 3D reconstructions, high-quality graphics and text in Turkish and English.

Today the museum visitor who makes it to the Ziyaret Tepe rooms is treated to a wealth of information about the site, the scientific process of archaeology and life in Assyrian Tušhan.

Of course, with such a complex process, there was plenty of editorial work and checking to be done. The initial text panels, while visually stunning, contained minor errors that needed to be corrected, ensuring that images of the cuneiform tablets were the right way up, that each photograph matched its caption, and so on. The museum and production staff worked meticulously and, with our co-operative efforts, together we ensured that the final galleries are a resounding success.

Right
Plan of the new museum in Diyarbakır, showing the arrangement of displays for the rooms dedicated to Ziyaret Tepe

'The museum and production staff worked meticulously and, with our co-operative efforts, together we ensured that the final galleries are a resounding success'

Above
Prof. Timothy Matney inspects the Ziyaret Tepe displays

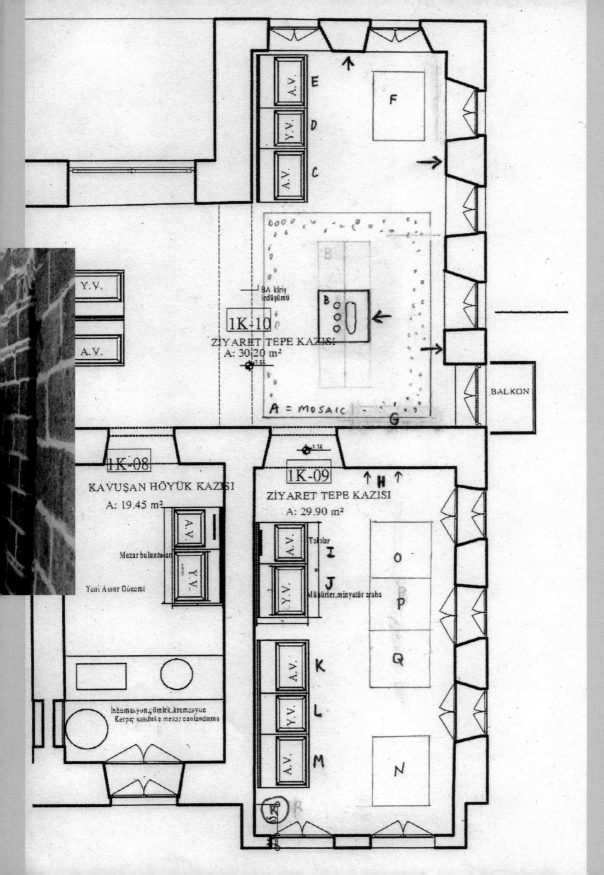

E A.V.

D Y.V.

C A.V.

F

Y.V.

A.V.

BA kiriş izdüşümü

1K-10

ZİYARET TEPE KAZISI
A: 30.20 m²

B

A = MOSAIC

G

BALKON

1K-08

KAVUŞAN HÖYÜK KAZISI
A: 19.45 m²

A.V.

Y.V.

Mezar buluntuları

Yeni Assur Dönemi

İnhumasyon,çömlek,kremasyon
Kerpiç sanduka mezar canlandırma

1K-09

ZİYARET TEPE KAZISI
A: 29.90 m²

H

A.V.

I

Y.V.

J

A.V.

K

Y.V.

L

A.V.

M

Tablolar

Mühürler,minyatür araba

O

P

Q

N

The end of the Assyrian Empire and the fall of Tušhan

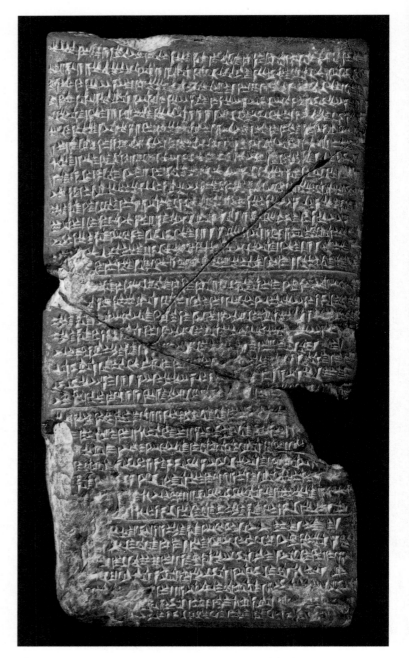

Following the death of Ashurbanipal in 627 BC the Assyrian Empire quickly began to unravel. With the population of the heartland diluted by deportees and the influx of Aramean tribes, with pressure on resources and factionalised by civil war, the disintegration of Assyria was to be predicted. The actual military overthrow was brought about by a coalition of Babylonians, Medes and Cimmerians.

From the death of Ashurbanipal to freefall collapse took just 15 years. The iconic event was the fall of Nineveh in 612 BC. A major source for this is the Babylonian Chronicle – damaged and incomplete, to be sure, but nevertheless an extraordinary witness to these events. According to the Chronicle, in the 14th year of Nabopolassar (first king of the Neo-Babylonian Empire), the king mustered his army and joined forces with Cyaxares (the Mede, from Iran) and the 'Umman-mandu' (Cimmerians, from around the Caucasus):

'They marched along the bank of the Tigris. They encamped against Nineveh. From the month of Sivan until the month of Ab, for three months, they subjected the city to a heavy siege. [On day x] of the month of Abu they inflicted a major defeat upon a great people. At that time

Above
The Babylonian Chronicle, damaged and incomplete though it is, records the end of the great Assyrian Empire, brought about by a coalition of Babylonians, Medes and Cimmerians

Sin-shar-ishkun king of Assyria died.'

Thus is recorded one of the most cataclysmic events of world history. Nevertheless, it was not quite the final end. For a few more years Assyria staggered on as a political entity, contracting into the northwest sector of the former Empire, centred on a capital at Harran. In the process the front line drew back across this region. In 611 BC it was the turn of Tušhan.

'In the 15th year, in the month of Tammuz, the king of Babylon [mustered his troops] and went to Assyria. [He marched about] imperiously [in Ass]yria and conquered the [citie]s of T[u]šha[n, ...] and Shu[br]ia. They took [their people] as captives and [carried away] a hea[vy] booty from them.'

At Ziyaret Tepe there is evidence for these events. On the archaeological side, it is clear that the monumental buildings were abandoned with sufficient time to remove any valuables. There is also evidence for burning, though it has not so far been possible to establish whether or not this was deliberate.

The evidence from the texts is more compelling. Most dramatic is the text ZTT 22, a letter written by a high official, Mannu-ki-libbali, who had evidently been asked to muster a unit of chariotry. However, the entire structure to support such an order had collapsed, and he writes back in despairing tones that the only possible outcome is death. This letter is unparalleled. It can only have been written as the front line drew close to Tušhan and the infrastructure of the Empire collapsed. As a first-hand account of Assyria in its death throes it is unique.

What happened to Tušhan, and indeed to the region as a whole, in the years following the disappearance of Assyrian government is not yet clear. It was once thought that Assyria was entirely wasted, but recent studies have shown that the level of devastation was less than total, and that many of the major cities continued in

One of the most extraordinary finds from Ziyaret Tepe is a letter written as the Assyrian Empire was in the very process of collapse. Written by an official named Mannu-ki-libbali, it details the woeful situation in Tušhan as centralised authority disintegrated:

'Concerning the horses, Assyrian and Aramean scribes, cohort commanders, officials, coppersmiths, blacksmiths, those who clean the tools and equipment, carpenters, bow-makers, arrow-makers, weavers, tailors and repairers, to whom should I turn? ...Not one of them is there. How can I command? ...The lists are not at my disposal. According to what can they collect them? Death will come out of it. No one [will escape]. I am done!'

at least a reduced manner. The Empire was carved up between the victors. The Medes took the Zagros territories, but the degree to which they were able to administer them is far from clear. The Babylonians, on the other hand, were the mainstream successors to the Assyrian Empire, taking over direct rule in Mesopotamia as far north as Assur, retaining the provinces in what is now modern Syria, reasserting control of Palestine and campaigning in the northwest.

In the case of Ziyaret Tepe it appears that there was squatter occupation for a limited period, after which the site was abandoned. It seems that with the disappearance of Assyrian power the infrastructure that had supported the region's prosperity simply disintegrated. Regional agricultural collapse followed.

As regards what happened to the population of Tušhan, we can only guess. It has to be imagined that many were killed, and that large numbers will have been enslaved as prisoners of war. Those of Assyrian descent may initially have fled towards Harran, to the closing act of the Empire which awaited them there. At least the more recent deportees and their descendants may have fled back to their homeland.

Director's epilogue

Eighteen years is a long time. When I left for Ziyaret Tepe for the first season in the summer of 1997, my children were three and one years old. When I got home at the end of the last season in 2014, my daughter was just starting her junior year and my son was a freshman in college. Hundreds of colleagues and workmen have worked tens of thousands of hours on the project. Scores of academic articles, hundreds of presentations, a few doctoral and master's dissertations, even a few marriages, have emerged from those long, hot, dusty days in southeastern Turkey. With all the toil and trouble, it's a fair question to ask what we have learned from all this labour.

First of all, we know that the ancient mound that lies a few kilometres east of the modern town of Tepe was once the provincial capital of the mighty Assyrian Empire, a place important

The hills of Shubria bathed in golden light

enough to house the governor and his administration, a place which the king and his army used as a starting point for their never-ending battles to keep the northern frontier of the Empire safe. We know its name, Tušhan, and can now connect historical references in the cuneiform record with an actual place. In fact, we think we have even found the very building that was referenced in those texts in the Bronze Palace on the citadel mound. We know that the powerful had beautiful luxury goods – gold, silver, precious stones, ivory and bronze. We know what they ate, how they decorated their buildings, where they stored the city's grain, and to whom it was dispensed. We know that they held ceremonies in their palace, where the dead were cremated, replete with their prized possessions, in a curiously un-Assyrian fashion.

We know where the soldiers stood guard in the city gate, playing at dice and warming themselves around a small hearth on cold winter evenings. The carts full of agricultural produce have left their ruts in the stone threshold leading into the city, and the flocks of animals brought into the city for safety or slaughter have left us their bones. We know that the commoners did not have the thickest cuts of meat, or the fanciest houses, or the finest ceramic vessels. They buried their

dead in simple pit graves beneath the floors of their houses with offerings of bead necklaces and perhaps pottery vessels containing food and drink. We know that not all the inhabitants were Assyrians; some were foreigners from lands where no written native language was recorded. Perhaps they were deportees brought as spoils of war to farm the fertile fields around Tušhan and fill its granaries.

Eighteen years is also such a short time. For all the questions we have answered about this ancient city, an even greater number remain unanswered. Were there markets and orchards and parks at Tušhan? If so, where? We know there must have been a temple in the city; in fact, we think it may have been dedicated to the goddess Ištar of Nineveh, but it remains elusive. Where did the inhabitants make their pottery? Who tended the herds?

The texts tell us that Tušhan in the Late Assyrian period was built upon an earlier Assyrian city called Tušhum, but that Middle Assyrian city is largely unexplored. In fact, we know that the high mound was occupied from long before this, during the Early and Middle Bronze Ages, but those periods are only known at Ziyaret Tepe from a few soundings. We have only scratched the top few metres of an enormous mound

22m high. Once I calculated, in a very rough manner, how long it would take to excavate the entire site at the rate we were working. I don't remember the exact figure, but it was well over a century. Eighteen years is indeed a short time!

I think that we can be satisfied, though, that we have a made a good start. Although the digging is done for now, there is a mountain of data left to be organised and analysed. A multi-volume final report is under way and the scientific study will continue in laboratories and offices across the globe as archaeologists, specialists and students pore over the vast archive of material laboriously recorded by the field team. There are certainly many discoveries left to be made, even if many of them will be less colourful and exciting than the ones we have presented in this book.

I often describe archaeology to my first-year students as the equivalent of working on a jigsaw puzzle without the picture on the front of the box as a guide, and with most of the pieces missing. Thanks to all the efforts of our Ziyaret Tepe team, we now have a few more pieces with which to work. Such success is entirely due to the tireless efforts of the excellent team of archaeologists and specialists who returned, summer after summer, to labour under the hot Turkish sun. I would like to extend here my unending thanks to all my team for their efforts, energy, goodwill and cheer, without which this undertaking would hardly have been possible.

A spectacular sunset silhouettes the mound of Ziyaret Tepe

Appendix A
A-Z of the operation areas

Operation A/N Broad clearance of the Bronze Palace, a monumental mud-brick building on the eastern side of the high mound dating to the Late Assyrian period. Excavations here were undertaken from 2000 to 2002 under the direction of Duncan Schlee (**Operation A**) and from 2007 to 2013 under the direction of Dirk Wicke (**Operation N**).

Operations B 5 x 5m sounding conducted in 2000 in order to investigate an anomaly appearing in the magnetometry survey; the excavation revealed Middle Islamic surfaces and a large tannur (bread oven).

Operation C 5 x 5m trench on the western slope of the high mound excavated in 2000 in a location where local villagers had removed a large stone the previous winter; remains of a well-preserved building of the early 2nd millennium BC were found.

Operation D The first operation in the lower town, carried out in 2000 under the direction of John MacGinnis, uncovering a section of the eastern city wall and associated architecture.

Operation E Step trench down the eastern slope of the high mound, and the principal stratigraphic investigation carried out at Ziyaret Tepe, excavated by Michael Roaf over 2000–04. This 5m-wide cut documented a series of occupation layers spanning the Early Bronze Age, the early 2nd millennium BC, and the Mitanni, Middle Assyrian, local Iron Age and Late Assyrian periods.

Operation F Salvage operation near the northern base of the mound examining the damage done by robbers using a backhoe in 2000 to cut through a thick deposit of slope wash of post-Assyrian date.

Operation G/R Extensive excavation in the western part of the lower town directed by John MacGinnis over the period 2001–13, revealing two major Late Assyrian buildings, an elite residence and an administrative building which housed an important archive of cuneiform tablets dating to the very end of the Empire. Both buildings were paved with beautiful mosaic pavement courtyards.

Operation H Brief exploration of a possible graveyard near the Tigris River north of the mound carried out in 2001. The graves were post-Assyrian and badly disturbed by modern activities.

Operation I Series of 1 x 2.5m test pits running along an east-west transect across the northern part of the high mound executed in 2001 by Michael Roaf. The purpose of this operation was to identify the nature of the stratigraphy on the high mound and to look for promising areas for future excavation.

Operation J Excavation of an area at the western edge of the lower town carried out by Monica Smith in 2002. Our attention had been drawn to the area by a concentration of Late Roman pottery and roof tiles, with excavation revealing a substantial Late Roman building superimposed upon earlier Late Assyrian remains.

Operation K Excavation at the southern city wall, carried out under the direction of Kemalettin Köroğlu in 2003–04 and again in 2013, which provided a detailed phasing of the wall and also uncovered a block of adjacent architecture tentatively identified as a barracks. This area produced our best evidence for non-elite life at Ziyaret Tepe.

Operation L Area located in the northwestern corner of the high mound, excavated in 2004 and 2006–2008 under the direction of Kemalettin Köroğlu, which produced the best-preserved remains from the Middle Islamic and Ottoman periods at the site, as well as an important sequence from the Hellenistic/Late Iron Age, the Late Assyrian period and the Early Iron Age.

Operation M Initially a small trench excavated in 2004 by Ann Donkin in order to ground-truth a feature appearing in all three forms of geophysics conducted at the site (resistivity, magnetometry and ground penetrating radar), which confirmed that the feature was a road, at the same time demonstrating the presence of adjoining mud-brick architecture. In 2012 work was resumed in the area by Kemalettin Köroğlu in order to further investigate this architecture, revealing part of a well-built domestic structure of the Late Assyrian period.

Operation N See Operation A.

Operation P 5 x 15m trench in the western lower town excavated in 2007 by David Kertai in order to investigate a prominent circular feature seen in the resistivity survey. While poorly preserved remnants of Late Assyrian surfaces were encountered, it was determined that the geophysical feature was compacted soil of modern origin.

Operation Q Excavation of the 'Khabur Gate', the main gate into the southern lower town, conducted in 2007–10 under the direction of John MacGinnis. The operation exposed an area of 400sq m and revealed a complete plan, over four phases of rebuilding, of | the Late Assyrian gate along with the roadway leading to it.

Operation R See Operation G.

Operation S 5 x 5m trench excavated in 2010 in a field outside of the southern city walls in order to investigate the purported presence of ancient graves. No significant finds were made.

Operation T Area in the lower town south of the high mound excavated in 2011 by Kemalettin Köroğlu, revealing domestic residences dating to the Late Roman and Late Assyrian periods, including evidence that the Assyrian building had, at one point, been levelled and rebuilt along nearly identical wall lines.

Operation U Excavation of a 100sq m area in the southeastern sector of the lower town carried out by John MacGinnis in 2011 discovering, as in **Operation T**, Late Roman occupation superimposed upon earlier phases of Assyrian domestic architecture.

Operation V Excavation near the **Operation Q** gate carried out in 2011 by John MacGinnis and Kristina Sauer in order to investigate a structure appearing in the geophysical survey which proved to be a well-preserved building with a cobbled surface of Late Assyrian date.

Operation W Targeted excavations carried out to elucidate two questions pertaining to the **Operation G/R** architectural complex, (i) to investigate whether certain features of larger stones set into the pebbled mosaic pavements marked the location of graves, and (ii) to establish the building's full sequence of construction phases.

Operation Y Investigation carried out in 2013 under the direction of Mary Shepperson at a location on the southwestern edge of the lower town where the geophysical mapping showed a sharp turn in the city wall. The excavation revealed that the turn was constructed as a smooth curve with concentric rows of bricks fanning out to make the bend; the work

also demonstrated that a strip 2.5m-wide was maintained as a clearway for communications on the inside of the wall.

Operation Z 5 x 5m sounding in the western lower town carried out in 2013 to ground-truth the existence of a large building whose presence was suggested by the geophysical survey. A substantial mud-brick wall dating to the Late Assyrian period was found at the expected location.

Appendix B
The team

Below are the names of 438 field participants at Ziyaret Tepe. Some were with us for only a few days or weeks, some for nearly two decades. Many names are missing, either because of mistaken omission or because they represent the large number of people who made up our support team in Turkey: museum directors and personnel, local shopkeepers and merchants, accountants and safety engineers, mayors, bankers and funders. Important, of course, is our even broader support network of family and friends back at home who kept everything running smoothly while we were in the field. The list is, quite literally, endless.

Ziyaret Tepe, the Scientific Team, 1997–2014

Karen Abend, Kaisa Akerman, Rıza Akgün, Zuhal Alcan, Guillermo Algaze, Adam Allentuck, Mesut Alp, Evelyn Alvarez-Dossman, David Astbury, Nahide Aydın, Peter Bartl, Daniela Arroyo Barrantes, Andrew Bauer, Celine Beauchamp, Jordan Bell, Remi Berthon, Tom Burns, Emily Cavalier, Esther Chao, Melanie Clifton-Havey, Ian J. Cohn, Harun Danışmaz, Tim Demko, Gülay Dinçkan, Laurent Dissard, Ann Donkin, David Dorren, Judith Dosch, Charlie Draper, Patricia Duff, Lauralee Elliot, Leomie Willoughby Ellis, Olga Emgrund, Nurşen Fındık, Lourdes Mesa Garcia, Bülent Genç, Jill Goulder, Haskel Greenfield, Tina Greenfield, Roberta Guarino, Julyana Gülten, Emily Hammer, Britt Hartenberger, Carl Hayward, Joseph Heigermoser, Birger Helgestad, Yvonne Helmholz, Fabian Heubel, Alex Hirtzel, Tara Hornung, Barbara Jakubowska, Chelsea Jalbrzikowski, Marie Brondegaard Jensen, Natalia Kadzidłowska, İbrahim Kars, Mustafa Kılıçal, Pinar Kaymakçı, Nuretdin Kaymakçı, Sara Kayser, David Kertai, Azer Keskin, Franziska Kierzek, Stephan Kintzel, Songül Kısıklı, Kemalettin Köroğlu, Ratko Krvavac, Nineb Lammasu, Christine Lincke, Sandra Lösch, Tom Lyons, John MacGinnis, Helen Malko, Çiğdem Maner, Timothy Matney, Helen McDonald, Hillary McDonald, Negahnaz Moghaddam, Friederike Moll-Dau, Hayley Monroe, Willis Monroe, Kathleen Nicoll, Gülşen Özek, Latif Özen, Raffaella Papalardo, Simo Parpola, Jonathan Pilgrim, Brian Pittman, Agnieszka Poniewierska, Lucas Proctor, Paola Pugsley, Christine Puza, Milo Reddaway, Mandy Reimann, Charlotte Rerolle, Simo Rista, Michael Roaf, Richard Roaf, Melissa Rosenzweig, Eric Rupley, Jane Sanford, Fabian Sarga, Kristina Sauer, Duncan Schlee, Guido Schnell, Monique Schröder, Mary Shepperson, Philipp Schmidt, Caroline Skelton, Monica Smith, Lewis Somers, Diana Stein-Wuenscher, Jason Stein-Wuenscher, Burhan Süer, Jim Sutter, Jeff Szuchman, Armağan Tan, Mehmet Tekin, Johanna Tudeau, Valentina Vezzoli, Tasha Vorderstrasse, Marcin Wagner, Jennifer Walborn, Dirk Wicke, Dominique Wiebe, Jerzy Wierzbicki, Ania Wodzinska, Fatoş Yaşar, Necmi Yaşar, Tuba Yaşar, Thomas Zimmerman.

Ziyaret Tepe, government representatives (temsilci), 1997–2014

Murat Ak, Murat Aktay, Zerrin Akdoğan, Leyla Ay, Esma Bedirhanoğlu, Melek Çanga, Nuray Çırak, Özgür Çomak, Sema Dayan, Hakan Dinç, Ahmet Durman, Nezammetin Kaya, Recep Okçu, Nevin Soyukaya, Eşref Sürücü, Nurhan Turan, Ertan Yılmaz, Yaşar Yılmaz.

Ziyaret Tepe, local workmen, 2000–2014

Bayram Akaydın, Hakkı Akaydın, Mehmet Selim Akaydın, Murat Akaydın, Musa Akaydın, Şeyhmus Akaydın, Yavuz Akaydın, Mehmet Salih Akgül, Şaban Akgül, Fatma Aktar, Betül Alican, Adnan Altay, Erdal Altun, Süleyman Altun, Mehmet Emin Altunbaş, Ahmet Altundere, Navaf Altundere, İslam Arslan, Vedat Arslan, Ali Artan, Sedat Artan, Engin Aslan, Sezgir Aslan, Hamdullah Avcı, Abdulgafur Avras, Şakir Avras, Abdullah Ayaz, Osman Ayaz, Resul Ayaz, Sabri Ayaz, Veysi Ayaz, Yahya Ayaz, Hasan Aydoğan, Kemal Aydoğan, İsa Şerif Aygün, Şirin Bakir, Aydin Bal, Halim Bal, Metin Bal, Murat Bal, Musa Bal,

Salih Bal, Abdulselam Balıkçı, Hikmet Balıkçı, Selim Balıkçı, Ayşe Başaran, Hamid Başaran, Serap Başaran, Mehmet Bayar, Cemil Baydur, Engin Baydur, Fatma Baydur, Resul Baydur, Vedat Baydur, Güven Biçim, Şahin Biçim, Mehmet Boğa, Abdullatif Bulut, Ahmet Bulut, Hayrettin Bulut, Mehmet Emin Bulut, Namık Bulut, Sait Bulut, Bekir Can, İslam Can, Servet Can, Vedat Can, Murat Cantekin, Abdulkadir Çelebi, Adem Çelebi, Ahmet Çelebi, Ekrem Çelebi, Halit Çelebi, Hüseyin Çelebi, İsa Çelebi, Kemal Çelebi, Mehmet Hasip Çelebi, Şaban Çelebi, Uğur Çelebi, Vedat Çelebi, Ahmet Çelik, Davut Çelik, İbrahim Çelik, Muharrem Çelik, Fadıl Çetin, Haydar Çetin, Mahsun Çetin, Mehmet Sedik Çetin, Müslim Çetin, Mustafa Çetin, Zübeyir Çetin, İsmail Çınar, Mehmet Emin Çınar, Hacı Dağlı, İrfan Dağlı, Adnan Demir, Mehmet Şah Demir, Ömer Demir, Rıza Demir; Salahattin Demir, Sinan Demir, Süleyman Demir, Vedat Demir, Yusuf Demir, Aydın Doğru, Dogan Doğru, Mehi Doğru, Meki Doğru, Şahin Doğru, Zeki Doğru, Emir Dünmez, Hamdullah

Dünmez, Abdulbaki Ekin, Abdullah Ekin, Abdulmenaf Ekin, Abdulvahap Ekin, Murat Ekin, Suat Ekin, Vedat Ekin, Abdulgafur Eroğlu, Medeni Eroğlu, Sedat Eroğlu, Kerim Filiz, Hikmet Firiz, Veysel Göl, İrfan Gözüaçık, Ahmet Güçlü, Mehmet Şirin Güçlü, Erhan Gül, Fikret Gül, Hakan Gül, Miktat Gül, Osman Gül, Nizamettin Gülaydın, Rıdvan Gülaydın, Mehmet Güldaş, Abdulrahman Gültekin, Arap Gültekin, Bünyamin Gültekin, Fatih Gültekin, İkram Gültekin; Mesut Gültekin, Muhittin Gültekin, Necmi Gültekin, Abdulrahman Gündüz, Ömer Gündüz, Şerif Güner, Vecdi Güner, Ahmet Güneş, Asım Güneş, Bünyamin Güneş, Fatih Güneş, Habib Güneş, Hamit Güneş, Hamza Güneş, Haydar Güneş, Mithat Güneş, Muhittin Güneş, Namuk Güneş, Şahin Güneş, Vahyettin Güneş, Mehmet Güven, Hasan Hasanoğlu, Mehmet Hasanoğlu, Mehmet İnanç, Muhittin İnanç, Tahsin İnanç, Metin İpek, Ayhan Işık, Şevki Işık, Abdulselam Kahraman, Mehmet Kahraman, Ömer Kahraman, Vecdi Kahraman, Şükrü Kalkan, Zeki Kalkan,

Süleyman Karabulut, Şehmus Karademir, İbrahim Karakoç, Ömer Karakoç, Ramazan Karakoç, Seyfettin Karakoç, Behzat Kartal, Hikmet Kartal, Murat Kartal, Ramazan Kartal, Sedat Kartal, İzzettin Kaya, Süphi Kaya, Ali Kızılkaya, Bozo Kızılkaya, Cundullah Kızılkaya, Hüsnü Kızılkaya, Mahsun Kızılkaya, Mustafa Kızılkaya, Siraç Kızılkaya, Talip Kızılkaya, Veysi Kızılkaya, Münür Korkmaz, Şaban Korkmaz, Mehmet Ali Kurt, Zeliha Kutlu, Edip Ok, Mehmet Zekri Ok, Ahmet Orhan, Suat Orhan, Baki Örs, Zikri Örs, Halef Ortaç, Arif Özaydın, Hakan Özaydın, Hamza Özaydın, Mehmet Necat Özaydın, Ramazan Özaydın, Saim Özaydın, Şeyhmus Özaydın, Selim Özaydın, Derviş Özbek, Hamit Özbek, Recep Özbek, İbrahim Özçelik, Abdullah Özdamar, Osman Özdamar, Halis Özdas, İbrahim Özkaya, Ayhan Sancar, İlhami Sancar, Mahmut Sancar, Mehmet Nuri Sancar, Mehmet Salih Sarı, Muas Sayılın, Cemal Sayılır, Abdulkadir Sevim, Bahattin Sevim, Seret Sevim, Ali Kadir Sümer, İsa Sümer, Mahsun Sümer, Şahin Sümer, Tarık Sümer,

İbrahim Sun, Mehmet Emin Sun, Rıfat Sun, İlhami Şeker, Mehmet Ali Şeker, Edip Şekerci, Kenan Şekerci, Halil Şimşek, Mehmet Şirin Şimşek, Zülkif Şimşek, Halil Tangüner, Ahmet Tanrıkulu, Cemalettin Tanrıkulu, Hasan Tanrıkulu, Kerem Tanrıkulu, Murat Tanrıkulu, Edip Taş, Adem Tunç, Behcet Tunç, Eşref Tunç, İsmet Tunç, Ahmet Turan, Cafer Turan, Ömer Turan, Aydın Turğay, Ramazan Uçar, Fatiha Uçar, Hamdin Uçar, Mecdi Uçar, Mecit Uçar, Medeni Uçar, Mehmet Uçar, Şeyhmus Üçlü, Aydın Yel, Ramazan Yer, Arslan Yıldız, Aslan Yıldız, Hayrettin Yıldız, Ömer Yıldız, Abdullah Yılmaz, Cihan Yılmaz, Maruf Yılmaz, Mehmet Salih Yılmaz, Şirin Yılmaz, Abdulkadir Yüksekdağ, Bahri Yüksekdağ, Fetih Yüksekdağ, Hanifi Yüksekdağ, Nihat Yüksekdağ, Ömer Yüksekdağ, Raşit Yüksekdağ, Şehmus Yüksekdağ, Ümit Yüksekdağ, Vahit Yüksekdağ, Enver Yüksel.

Index

Index

228

Sponsors

It is a pleasure and honour to acknowledge our debt and gratitude to all the many generous sponsors without whom the work at Ziyaret Tepe would not have been possible:

Erhan Öner
Ercan Kumcu
Feyyaz Berker
Tekfen Foundation

The American Philosophical Society, the American Research Institute in Turkey, Houshang Ardavan, the Assyrian community of Botkyrka, the Assyrian community of Gothenberg, the Assyrian Foundation of America, Nicholas Baring, Fenella Barton, Jane Beatty, Graeme Barker, Richard Barker, Peter Beckwith, Michael Behrman, Richard and Ann Behrman, Sir Leszek Borysiewicz, Curtiss T and Mary G Brennan Foundation, the British Institute of Archaeology in Ankara, the British School of Archaeology in Iraq, Lord Browne of Madingley, Robin Chapman and Sarah-Jane Marshall, Peggy and Dave Chenoweth, Sir Ian Cheshire, Dr J S Cohen, Penny Cotton, Ted and LaVaughn Craig, Stephanie Dalley, the Deutsche Forschungsgemeinschaft, Vicky Few, Dr Eden Frye in memory of Donny George, Clive and Etsuko Galliver, Betsy Garrett, Simon and Tracy Gleeson, David Goldstone, the Guinness family, John Hamilton and Carol Leonard, David Harding, Dr David and Margaret Hartnett, John and Liz Heard, Simon and Alex Hirtzel, Adrian and Archie Hogarth, the Institute for the Study of the Ancient World, Michael Jary, Linda Jayne, Richard and Susan Jebb, the Johannes Gutenberg-Universität Mainz, the Koç Foundation, Neil Kreitman, Linda Laine, Alyona Ledeneva, Laura Lloyd, Sir Timothy Lloyd, Tom Macey-Dare, Carolyn MacGinnis, Lise Madsen and Adrian Apodoca, Shamiran Mako, the McDonald Institute for Archaeological Research, Mednick Grant from the Virginia Foundation of Independent Colleges, John Michael, Marina Michaels, Carolyne Mitchell-Innes, James Mosse, the National Endowment for the Humanities, the National Geographic Society, the National Science Foundation, Katherine Pakenham, Charles Pettiward, Roger and Nadine Pilgrim, the Polonsky family, J N Postgate, the Priestley family, James and Grace Rankin, Sir Hans Rausing, Sir Alec Reed, Lord Renfrew of Kaimsthorn, the Römisch Germanisches Zentralmuseum, Bridget Rose, Sir Evelyn de Rothschild, Sir Timothy Sainsbury, William Scaldwell, Bernard Selz, Nenos Shemoon, John and Bellinda Spillane, Peter Stevens, Sweet Briar College, Sir Peter Swinnerton-Dyer, Trinity College, Cambridge, Sir Anthony Touche, the University of Akron, the University of Cambridge, the University of Minnesota, Duluth, Peter and Monica Unwin, David and Grizelda Vermont, the G A Wainwright Fund, the Wasserstein family, Chikako Watanabe, the Wenner-Gren Foundation for Anthropological Research, Martina West, Mark Woodhouse, the Worshipful Company of Mercers, the Worshipful Company of Skinners, and the many trusts and foundations which supported the work through the Ziyaret Tepe Archaeological Trust.

Tekfen Foundation is the proud sponsor of Ziyaret Tepe Excavations and the publishing of this book.

TEKFEN FOUNDATION

Imprint

Design
Clive Crook
and Debi Angel
Text editor
Hilary Stafford-Clark

Project Coordinator
Dori Kiss Kalafat

Printed by
Ofset Yapımevi
Çağlayan, Şair Sok. No:4,
34403 Kağıthane/İstanbul
T: +90 212 295 86 01
Certificate No: 12326

Text © Timothy Cecil Matney, John MacGinnis, Dirk Wicke, Kemalettin Köroğlu

A Cornucopia Book
Published by Caique Publishing Ltd, 2017
1 Rutland Court,
Edinburgh EH3 8EY
in association with
Kayık Yayıncılık Ltd
Valikonağı Caddesi 64,
Nişantaşı, 34367 Istanbul

ISBN 978-0-9565948-9-1
ISBN 978-605-83080-2-2
Cornucopia Books
PO Box 13311,
Hawick, Scotland TD9 7YF

www.cornucopia.net

2017